STORY AND ART BY

MAKOTO RAIKU

THE STORY THUS FAR

The battle to determine who will be the next king of the mamodo world takes place every 1,000 years in the human world. Each mamodo owns a "book" which increases its unique powers and they must team up with a human in order to fight for their own survival. Zatch is one of 100 mamodo chosen to fight in this battle, and his partner is Kiyo, a junior high school student. The bond between Zatch and Kiyo deepens as they continue to survive through many harsh battles. Zatch swears, "I will fight to become a kind king."

After defeating the evil Zofis and his minions, Zatch and his friends return home. They soon meet a new mamodo, Ted, who makes friends with Zatch and ends up staying at Kiyo's house. In return for letting him stay there, Ted helps defend Zatch when a strange mamodo, Arth, attacks him. Ted and Zatch force Arth to retreat, but he leaves behind many mysteries. What is the secret of Zatch's spell "Bao Zakeruga"? What is the "menace of the mamodo world"? And what about the mysterious mamodo building which has appeared on Earth...?

PONYGON
A mamodo who stays at Kiyo's house. He finally found a book owner!
JIDO
Ted's partner. He's training Ted to be tough.
KAFK SUNBEAM
Ponygon's book owner who somehow understands what Ponygon is saying...! He works as an engineer in Japan.
TED
A mamodo who is looking for a girl mamodo, Cherish, who is precious to him. He and Zatch are friends.
DR. RIDDLES
He knows everything... or not. He used to be partners with Kedo, a mamodo who is now gone.
SUZY MIZUNO
A classmate who likes Kiyo. She's a kind girl who's naturally spacey and always gets mixed up in trouble.
KIYO'S CLASSMATES
ZEON
A mysterious mamodo who looks just like Zatch. For some reason he has stolen Zatch's memories of the mamodo world...!
IWA-SHIMA
A funny guy.
YAMA-NAKA
On the baseball team.

ZATCHBELL! 19

CONTENTS

LEVEL 173: I'm Not a Coward

CHOMP
MMM! MMM!
CHOMP
MUNCH
GULP
MMM! MMM!
CHOMP

MMM... MMM...
SIZZZ
SIZZ
MMM
GULP

YUMMY!
YOU'RE A GENIUS WHEN IT COMES TO MAKING FRIED EGGS, MA'AM!
THEY'RE NOT EVEN BURNT! THESE ARE THE BEST FRIED EGGS I'VE EVER HAD IN MY LIFE!
PLEASE MAKE ME SOME MORE!
HEY, TED! HOW MANY EGGS HAVE YOU EATEN ALREADY? DON'T YOU THINK THAT'S ENOUGH?
WHAP

SHUT UP. YOU'VE EATEN A LOT TOO, JIDO!
MY BODY IS MUCH BIGGER THAN YOURS, ALL RIGHT?
THAT'S OKAY.
EAT AS MUCH AS YOU WANT. YOU WON'T BE ABLE TO GET A HOME-COOKED MEAL WHEN YOU'RE BACK ON YOUR JOURNEY, WILL YOU?
CLANK
THANK YOU, MA'AM!
THANK YOU!
MNCH
CHMP
GULP
GULP

WELL, THANKS FOR LETTING US STAY.
SURE, THANKS FOR SAVING US LAST NIGHT.

YOU SHOULD PRACTICE FIGHTING AT CLOSE RANGE, ZATCH.
IT'LL MAKE YOU A LOT STRONG-ER!
WSH
WSH
OKAY, I WILL!
ONE MORE THING...
IF YOU EVER SEE A MAMODO NAMED CHERISH...
...TELL HER THAT TED WAS LOOK-ING FOR HER...
GRIP

TELL HER THAT I'M NOT HER ENEMY...

OKAY, I WON'T FIGHT AGAINST HER EITHER.
I'LL SEE IF I CAN FIND OUT ANYTHING ABOUT HER.
WE'RE TAKING OFF! THANKS, KIYO.
VRRRMM
DON'T LET ANYONE BEAT YOU, OKAY, ZATCH?

LET'S SURVIVE, AND HANG OUT AGAIN!
OKAY!
LET'S MEET AGAIN!
RRRRRMMMM

TWO DAYS LATER
HMM... SO THAT'S WHAT HAPPENED...

IT SOUNDS LIKE THE ENEMY COULD ATTACK US AT ANY TIME...
WELL ...

THE REASON I ASKED YOU TO COME HERE IS THAT...
I WANTED TO LET YOU KNOW THAT I'M GOING TO HOKKAIDO FOR A WEEK OF TRAINING.

I NEED YOU TO TAKE CARE OF PONYGON WHILE I'M AWAY.
MERU ?!

THIS TRAINING WILL BE TOUGH, AND...
...I'M NOT GOING TO BE ABLE TO TAKE PONYGON WITH ME THIS TIME.

IF I WERE TO GET ATTACKED BY AN ENEMY DURING MY TRAINING, I'D BE IN TROUBLE.
AS YOU SAID, WE MIGHT BE IN DANGER...

WOULD YOU TAKE CARE OF HIM FOR ME?
OF COURSE! DON'T WORRY ABOUT A THING!

WE'LL PROTECT YOU, PONYGON!
MERU ...

MERU MERU MERU MERU MERU MERU MERU!
I CAN'T TAKE YOU WITH ME, PONYGON.
PAT PAT
YOU'LL BE SAFER IF YOU STAY WITH ZATCH AND KIYO.

DON'T WORRY. I'LL BRING YOU BACK SOME TASTY HAY, OKAY?
MERU ...

ALL RIGHT, I'M OFF!
DOMF
ME...

SHOOOM
MERU-MERU-ME~

MERU~ MERU~ MERU MERU~
AWW, PONYGON. DON'T CRY.

MERU ~
COME ON, PONYGON. WE'RE GOING HOME.

HOKKAIDO

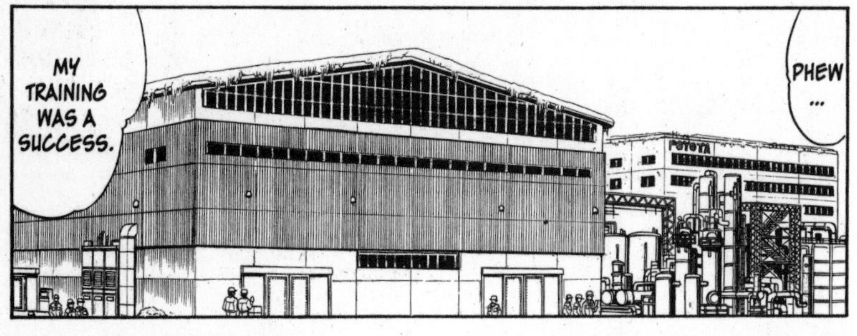
PHEW ...
MY TRAINING WAS A SUCCESS.

GREAT JOB, SUNBEAM. ARE YOU GOING HOME?
UH, NO... I'M GONNA GO BUY SOME SOUVENIRS. OH, I ALMOST FORGOT!
IS THERE ANYWHERE I CAN BUY TASTY HAY?
HAY...? YOU'RE KIND OF STRANGE ...
IF YOU GO TO A FARM IN THE SUBURBS, THEY MIGHT HAVE SOME.
THANKS.
VROOOM

DOOOOM

IT'S BIG ...
YEAH, THIS IS WHAT THEY CALL A HAY ROLL...

WE MAKE THESE DURING THE SUMMER, SO THAT WE CAN PRESERVE IT FOR THE HORSES TO EAT DURING WINTER WHEN THERE'S NO HAY.
YOU THINK YOU CAN TAKE THIS HOME?

I DON'T THINK SO.
WELL, I THOUGHT YOU MIGHT SAY THAT.

WHY DON'T YOU PUT AS MUCH AS YOU NEED IN THE SACK?
YOU'RE FUNNY, SO I'M NOT GONNA CHARGE YOU.

THANKS.
SHF
SHF

AHH... HOKKAIDO IS SOOOO HUGE!
THE HORSES LOOK SO HAPPY IN THIS HUGE, WIDE OPEN LAND!

TMPA TMPA TMPA
AH, THE HORSES ARE RUNNING TOWARDS ME!
OH, MY HORSES LOVE PEOPLE.
TMPA TMPA TMPA
DON'T BE SCARED.
THEY'RE ALL NICE!

TMPA TMPA TMPA TMPA

TMPA TMPA
TMPA TM PA

MPATMPA
PONYGON?!
TMPA
MERUIMERUIME~!

MERU-MERU-ME~!
LEAP
WAH!

AGGH!
TMPA
OH NO!
TM
TM
TMPA
HEY! STOP, YOU GUYS!
TM
PA
MERU-MERU-ME~!

PONYGON...
WHAT ARE YOU DOING HERE?

MERU-MERU-ME~ MERU-MERU-ME~!
OKAY, PONYGON. I UNDERSTAND.

IF YOU REALLY WANT TO GO TO HOKKAIDO, YOU SHOULD GO!
I SNEAK INTO KIYO'S SCHOOL ALL THE TIME, YOU KNOW?

*SIGN=RYUKYU (IN SOUTH JAPAN, THE OPPOSITE DIRECTION FROM HOKKAIDO)

Z Z Z
Z Z Z Z
MERU-MERU-ME~ MERU-MERU-ME~!
HUH?
OH, SORRY, PONYGON. I GUESS I'M PRETTY TIRED...

ANYWAY, WE'RE HAPPILY REUNITED, SO...
WHY DON'T WE GO DO SOME SIGHT-SEEING?
HA HA HA HA HA HA!
MERU-MERU-ME~
MRSH MRSH
SIZZLE

AHA HA HA HA HA!
MERU-MERU-ME~
AHA HA HA HA HA!
MERU-MERU-ME~E!
ROLL ROLL
HA HA HA HA HA HA!
MERU-MERU-ME~

SHIVER SHIVER
SHIVER SHIVER
AH, SORRY, PONYGON. I GOT CARRIED AWAY!
WAIT HERE, I'LL GO GET YOU SOME HOT MILK!
WHP
MERU-MERU-ME~

SHIVER SHIVER SHIVER
MERU~
MERU~
!!
...

FWIP
VWA

ME...
Tp
Tp
MERU-MERU...
SO YOU SENSED US BY DETECTING OUR ENERGY...
SHF...
I THOUGHT YOU WERE JUST A DUMB MAMODO, BUT...

LOOKS LIKE YOU HAVE SOME FIGHTING INSTINCTS...

MERU~
ME...
ME...
ME...
SHOOO

MERU ...

SNIFF
SNIFF

PARU-PARU-MONNN.
HMM ...

HE SAYS HE SMELLS ANOTHER MAMODO ON YOUR BODY.

ARE YOU WITH ANOTHER MAMODO?
ME ... MERU ...

I SEE ...

YOU'RE A MAMODO WHO CAN'T FIGHT WHEN YOU'RE ALONE, EH?
GGGGGGG

KARUDIO AND I ***HATE*** THOSE KINDS OF MAMODO...
IS YOUR FRIEND HERE WITH YOU?
ME...

NO, HE ISN'T!
TA
DA
PONYGON IS HERE BY HIMSELF!
I'M PONYGON'S PARTNER...
KAFK SUNBEAM!

HA, HA, HIS NAME IS PONYGON, HUH? NOT ONLY DOES HE LOOK STUPID, HIS NAME'S STUPID, TOO!

MY NAME IS SAUZAA.
MY MAMODO'S NAME IS KARUDIO.

UNLIKE PONYGON, HE'S GOT A COOL NAME, DOESN'T HE?
ME...
MERU-MERU-MERU-MERU-MERU-MERU-ME~!
My real name is SCHNEIDER!
DON'T YOU DARE SAY THAT!

WSH
PONYGON IS A FINE, UPRIGHT NAME!
DON'T MAKE FUN OF THE NAME HIS PARENTS GAVE HIM.
ME...
AND YOU MAKE IT SOUND LIKE HAVING FRIENDS IS SOMETHING BAD...
BUT YOU'RE WRONG...
FRIENDSHIP IS AN AMAZING THING THAT GIVES YOU EMOTIONAL SUPPORT.
ZAM
IF YOU THINK SOMEBODY'S A COWARD BECAUSE HE HAS A FRIEND, YOU'RE DEAD WRONG!
PONYGON HAS THE COURAGE TO FIGHT BY HIMSELF!

I JUST DON'T WANT YOU TO MISUNDERSTAND THAT...
GWOOOOOOOOO

LEVEL 174: Come Back Safe

GO GET HIM, PONYGON!
TM
MERU-MERU-ME~!
MERU-MERU-ME~!
KNG KNG KNG
GNG
PARU-PARU-MONN!

...
HEH
My real name is SCHNEIDER!
SO HIS REAL NAME IS SCHNEIDER...
BUT NOW HE'S CALLED PONYGON ...
GYOOM GNG

HA HA HA ...

ACTUALLY, HIS PARTNER LOOKS PRETTY STUPID TOO...
HUH?!
PARU-PARU-MONN!

HA!
DON'T MAKE ME LAUGH!

YOU CAN BARELY EVEN COMMUNICATE WITH EACH OTHER!
GN
BAP
I'M SURPRISED YOU MANAGED TO SURVIVE WITHOUT EVEN UNDERSTANDING EACH OTHER.
BANG

WH-WHAT ARE YOU SAYING?
PONYGON AND I HAVE AN EMOTIONAL CONNECTION!

COME ON, PONYGON!
SHOW THEM WHAT A GREAT COMBO WE MAKE!

I'VE BEEN PREPARING A STRATEGY FOR A FIGHT JUST LIKE THIS!
IT'S CALLED "PROJECT A"!
MERU-MERU-ME~!
"LISTEN, PONYGON... WE'RE GONNA USE A FEINT..."
"I'LL DO SOMETHING TO GET THE ENEMY'S ATTENTION, AND THEN WE'LL ATTACK THEM WHILE THEY'RE DISTRACTED!"

HAA!
PARU-PARU-MONN!
FLIP
MERU~~~~~~!
BAM
TA-DA

HA HA HA! WHAT A LAUGH!
THEY'VE GOT NO CONNECTION AT ALL!
...
DARN IT!
I SHOULDN'T HAVE DEPENDED ON SOME DUMB TRICK!
WHOMP

LET'S JUST FIGHT LIKE WE ALWAYS DO, PONYGON!
FASH
GO SHU-DORUK!
SHA
KEEEEEN

HMPH.
COME ON, KARUDIO!
GWOOOO
GO GIDO-RUK!
KEN KE.
SHA
BO
MERU-MERU-ME~!
OOM
BAKOOOM
MERU?

I GOT HIM, PARU!
HYOOOM
PONYGON!
!!

FWSHH
DGOOOM

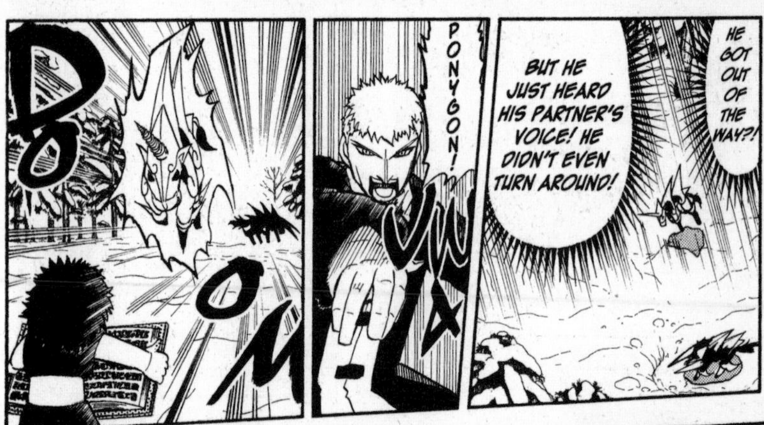
HE GOT OUT OF THE WAY?!
BUT HE JUST HEARD HIS PARTNER'S VOICE! HE DIDN'T EVEN TURN AROUND!
PONYGON!
DOOM
VWWAA

GRR! HE'S GOING AFTER MY PARTNER!
PARU-PARU-MONN!
DOOM
PONYGON!
BWAAM
PARU?!
SHWIP

PARUOOOOOOOOOO!
GROOVY!

WH-WHAT'S GOING ON? THEY'RE PER-FECTLY IN TUNE!
ARE THEY THE SAME PAIR WHO LOOKED SO STUPID JUST MOMENTS AGO?

DON'T UNDERESTIMATE THE COMBINATION TECHNIQUE THAT...
...HELPED US SURVIVE THE BATTLE AGAINST THE 1,000 YEAR-OLD MAMODO.

PONYGON!
TAKE THE BOOK AWAY FROM THE BOOK OWNER!

MERU-MERU!
FWOOM

ME...?!

WHAT?!
WHERE'D THEY GO?!

HEH... YOU SURE DID SURPRISE US, BUT...
DON'T THINK YOU'VE WON YET!

OUR CONNECTION IS JUST AS STRONG AS YOURS, AND OUR **ATTACK** IS AS STRONG AS YOURS, TOO!
HOW DID THEY GET THERE SO FAST...?!
WE'RE MUCH MORE ADVANCED THAN YOU ARE.
CAN YOU...

FWIP
...DO THIS?

FASH
DIOGIKOR GIDORUK!

KRIK
KRIK

!!?
KRIK
HYOOOOO
KRIK
SNAP

THE TREES AROUND US ARE FROZEN!
HYOOOO

THIS ISN'T LIKE THE OTHER POWER-UP SPELLS THEY'VE BEEN USING...
WHAT IS THIS?

HMPH... THIS IS A POWERFUL SPELL THAT EVEN SURPRISED ME.
THIS SPELL IS SO DANGEROUS THAT, AT FIRST, IT HURT ME WHENEVER I USED IT.

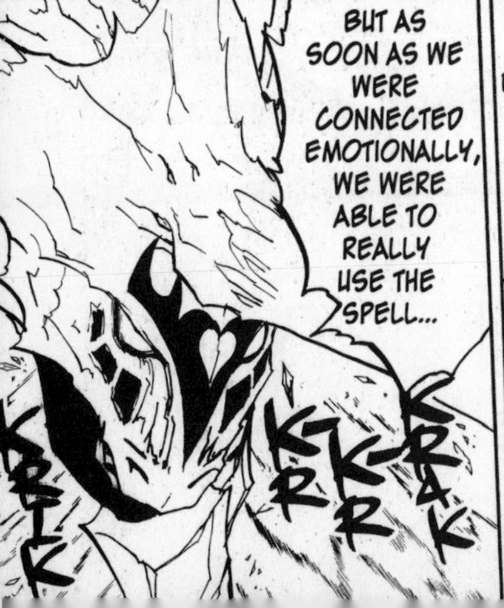
BUT AS SOON AS WE WERE CONNECTED EMOTIONALLY, WE WERE ABLE TO REALLY USE THE SPELL...
KRAK
KRRR

AND IT BECAME THE MOST INVINCIBLE SPELL IMAGINABLE!
HYOOOOOOU

IT LOOKS LIKE HIS BODY IS WRAPPED IN FREEZING COLD AIR...

!!
TA TM
MERU-MERU-ME--!

NO, PONYGON! DON'T TOUCH HIM!

SKRASH

KRIK
KRAK
KRIK
ME...
KRK
SNK

MERU-MERU-ME~!
BA
KYAAA

WHAT?!
HE SMASHED THE MIGHTY HORN OF GO SHUDORUK JUST LIKE THAT!
DID HE FREEZE PONYGON'S HORN, AND THEN SNAP IT LIKE AN ICICLE?!
IS HIS AURA OF FREEZING AIR REALLY THAT POWERFUL?!

ME...
MERU-MERU-ME~!
DOOM
NO, PONYGON! COME BACK!
HE'S TOO TOUGH FOR YOU TO FIGHT RIGHT N-

TNNG
KANGKANG
PARU-PARU-MONN!!!
MERU-MERU-ME~!
KLANG

PONYGON!
THWAMM
TMP
HMPH.

SEE? WITHOUT HIS FRIENDS TO GIVE HIM A HAND, HE'S HELPLESS.
THERE'S NO WAY HE CAN DEFEAT US... WE'VE BEEN TRAINING ALL THIS TIME BY OURSELVES SO WE COULD SURVIVE ON OUR OWN...
ARE YOU READY, KARUDIO?
LET'S GET HIS PARTNER AND BURN HIS BOOK!
ZAAA

!!
GRAB
MERU... ME... MERU...
...
HMPH... YOUR HANDS MUST BE FREEZING... I BET YOU CAN'T FEEL A THING.
BRR
BRRRRBR

WHY DON'T YOU JUST GIVE UP?
YOU'VE LOST! ADMIT IT!
KA
BAP
NOW GIVE ME THE BOOK!
DOOM
RRG...
AGGGH!
GYOOOO

GRAB
WHA-?!
WHY YOU...
SKIDDDD
"PONY-GON..."
"I'LL BE WAITING FOR YOU AT HOME, SO..."

"PROMISE ME YOU'LL COME BACK SAFELY."
SHIVER SHIVER
MERU ~~!
SHIVER
SHIVER

GRRR...
CUT IT OUT...

THAT'S RIGHT, WE CAN'T GIVE UP NOW!
I'VE GOT TO GET A LITTLE DISTANCE SO THAT PONYGON CAN CAST ANOTHER SPELL...!
DASH

GWOOOOOO
GWOOOO
THIS BATTLE IS OVER!
AH...

AGGGGHH!
IT'S SO COLD...! I CAN'T MOVE MY LEGS...OR MY BODY...!
DSSSHH
MERU~~~!
KRKRKRAKL
GWOOOO

ME... RU...
BIKI
"PROMISE ME...YOU'LL COME BACK SAFELY..."
BIKI
BIKI
"PROMISE ME..."
SNAP
KRAKL
MERU...
STING

"...YOU'LL COME BACK SAFELY!"
GW
OOOO
MERU~~~~!

!!
FWAAA

THE BOOK IS GLOWING ...
COULD IT BE...

...A NEW SPELL?
FWAAAA

HMPH! WHY DON'T YOU FREEZE TO DEATH?

OR I'LL WARM YOU UP... BY BURNING YOUR BOOK!
DOOM

DIOEMUR SHUDORUK!
FA
SH

KA-KOOOOOM

HA HA!
I KNEW IT! WE'RE WAY STRONGER THAN THEM! AWESOME!
CHWOOO

OKAY, WE'RE GONNA RIP THE BOOK FROM HIS FROZEN BODY...
!!
SPLASH

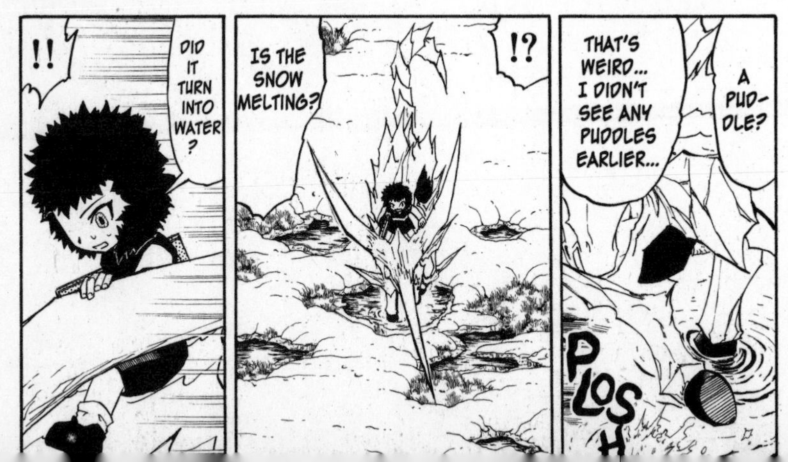
A PUD-DLE?
THAT'S WEIRD... I DIDN'T SEE ANY PUDDLES EARLIER...
PLOSH
!?
IS THE SNOW MELTING?
DID IT TURN INTO WATER?
!!

HWOOOOO
NO WAY!!!

PONY...
...GON....
OOOOO

LEVEL 175: Ignite Your Fighting Spirit!

LEVEL 175:
Ignite Your
Fighting Spirit!
KA
FWOOOMM

ZOOOOM
ZOOM
MERU...
GRRR

KREAKKKK
MERU-MERU-ME~!

MERU-MERU-ME~!
WAIT, KARUDIO, HE ISN'T-
PARU!

RRG...
BOOM
SHAAAA
SPLASH
PONY ... GON ...
AHH... IT'S WARM...
FSSH
FSSH
FSSH

MY HANDS AND LEGS WERE NUMB, BUT...
I CAN KIND OF MOVE THEM NOW...

!!

TOO HOT!
GASP
PONYGON, I'M ON FIRE!
KRAK
KRAK
POP
ME-MERU-MERU!
AGGGGGH...
SPLASH
SPLASH

HEH ...
HA HA HA!
JUST AS I EXPECTED... THEY'VE GAINED A NEW SPELL...
...BUT THEY CAN'T CONTROL IT!

I'M ICE AND YOU'RE FIRE!
EVEN THOUGH OUR POWERS ARE DIFFERENT, THE SPELLS ARE CONTROLLED THE SAME WAY!
IT'S JUST LIKE THE SPELL I'M USING NOW. IF YOU DON'T USE IT WITH GREAT CAUTION, YOU CAN PUT YOUR PARTNER IN DANGER!

MERU?
WHAT?!
WE HAD TO GO THROUGH TOUGH TRAINING AND STRENGTHEN OUR EMOTIONAL CONNECTION...
...SO THAT THE FREEZING AIR WON'T HURT ME WHEN I SIT ON KARUDIO'S BACK!
FWOOO

EVEN IF YOU TRY USING YOUR SPELL...
A-FWO
YOU'RE JUST GOING TO END UP BURNING YOUR PARTNER!

ME-MERU-MERU-ME~!
HRKORAK
AGGGH!
ME-?
URYAAAAAH!!!
KRASH
MERU-MERU-ME~!

ME-MERU-MERU~!
GWOOO
TSK, TSK!
BAD MAMODO! YOU'RE HURTING YOUR PARTNER!
ME...
GWOOO

THWAK
MERU~!
HA HA HA! NOT SO EASY TO CONTROL, IS IT?
MERU ...
MERU ...

PONY-GON...
ME...

DON'T WORRY ABOUT ME... JUST KEEP FIGHTING ...
THE BOOK IS GONNA BE FINE.
KIYO TOLD ME BEFORE THAT A MAMODO CAN'T BURN ITS OWN BOOK...

SO NO MATTER HOW HOT YOUR FLAMES ARE, YOUR BOOK WILL BE SAFE.
GO OUT THERE AND GIVE IT TO HIM GOOD!

HA HA HA! GIVE IT TO WHO?
MERU-MERU-ME~!
WHAMM

ME... MEME....
GWOOOO

PONYGON, I CAN ALSO CONTROL THE FLAME BY CONTROLLING MY STRENGTH FROM WITHIN!
I'LL CONTROL THE POWER OF THE FLAME ALONG WITH YOU. SO DON'T WORRY! JUST KEEP FIGHTING!
HA HA, WHAT THE HECK ARE YOU TALKING ABOUT?
YOU SOUND LIKE YOU'RE ABOUT TO PASS OUT!

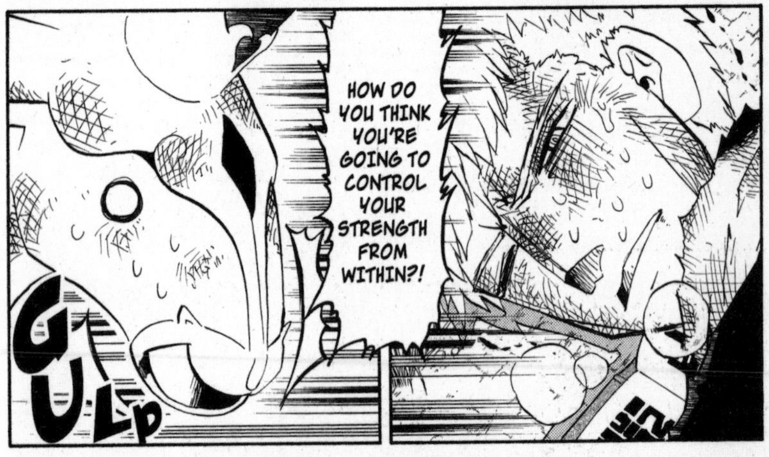
HOW DO YOU THINK YOU'RE GOING TO CONTROL YOUR STRENGTH FROM WITHIN?!
GULP

RRGG...
PONYGON!
!!
!!!

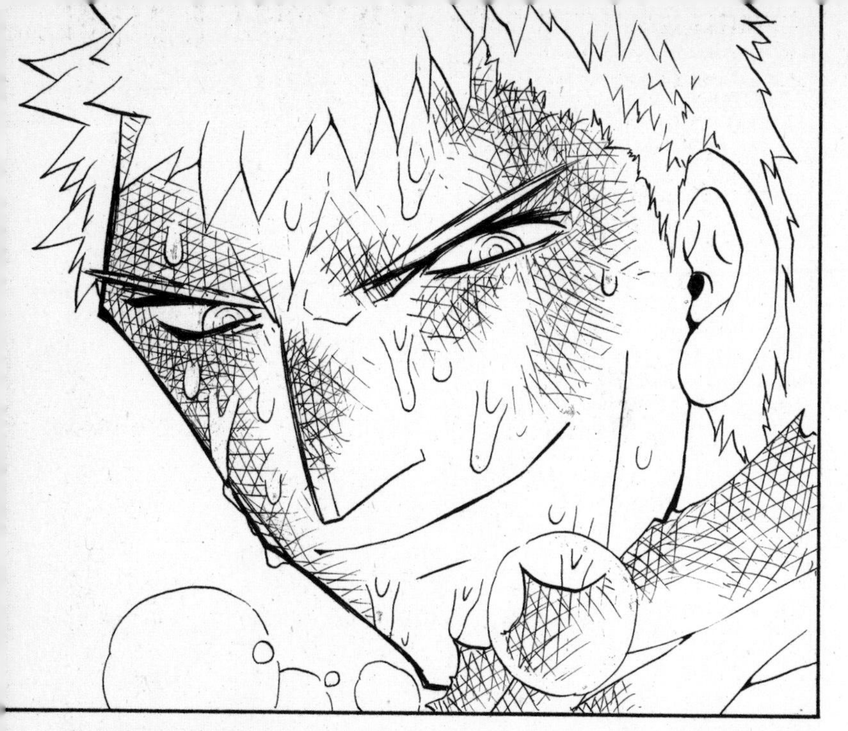

I'M NOT YOUR ENEMY, PONY-GON.
UNGH...
DON'T WORRY ABOUT ME.

FOCUS ON DEFEAT-ING HIM.
JUST LOOK INTO HIS EYES.

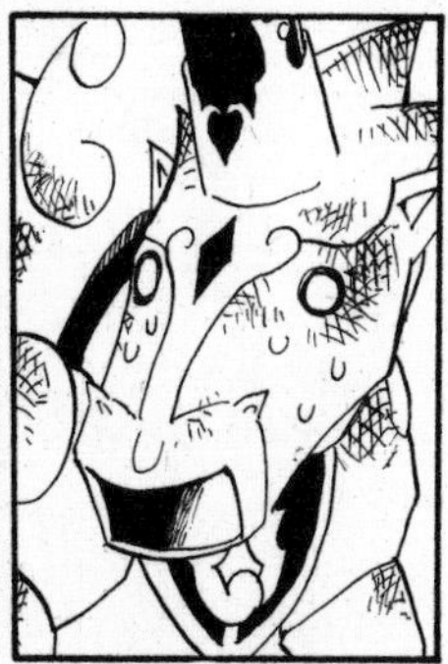

OUR BATTLES AREN'T ABOUT TECH-NIQUE...

DID YOU FOR-GET?
AND CONTROLLING THE FLAMES WON'T BE THAT HARD.

GOT IT?

IT'S ABOUT WHAT'S IN HERE.
TAP

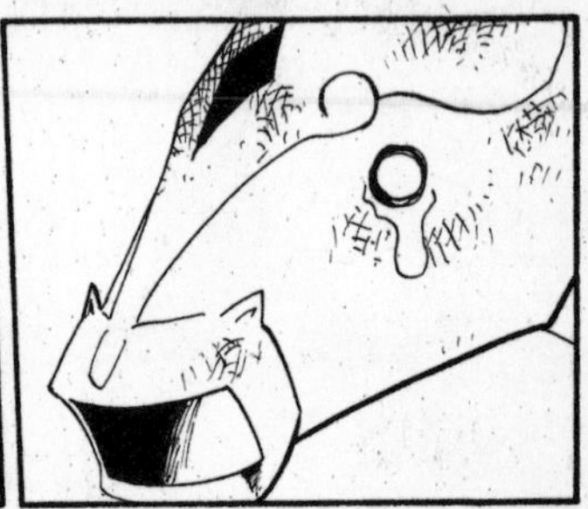

HA, YOU'RE TALKING NONSENSE!
THIS IS IT! IT'S ALL OVER!
DOM

LET'S DO THIS, PONY-GON.
ZATCH AND KIYO ARE WAITING FOR US...

MERU-MERU ME~!
FWSH

KRASH
KRAKL
KA
TUMP

ME...
MERU MERU!

BAM BAM
SKRASSH

ME...

MERU...

MERU...

ME... RU...

KARUDIO ...
NGH
NNGH
YOU'RE NOT HOLDING BACK, ARE YOU?
PARU ...
THEN WHY ...

WHY DON'T YOU FINISH HIM OFF ALREADY?
THA
WHAM

ARE YOU READY, KARUDIO?
TMP
WE'RE GONNA BURN THEIR BOOK.
PARU...
!!

GYOOOO
"JUST LOOK INTO HIS EYES."
"FOCUS ON DEFEATING HIM."

KA
FW
"IT'S ABOUT WHAT'S IN HERE!"
FOOOM
!!!

PARUUU?!!
NO WAY! HOW CAN HE CHARGE US AGAIN?!
COME ON, KARUDIO! COUNTER ATTACK!
KARUDIO!
PA...

PARUIMONN!!!
BYOOOOO

GH...
WHA-?!
FWOOOO

THIS IS JUST A FAKE BODY...
FSSHHHHH

HOW CAN HE CONTROL THE FLAME SO WELL? HE JUST LEARNED THIS SPELL!
...MADE OF FLAME?
VWSH
WHERE IS HE? WHERE'S HIS REAL BODY?
HE'S GONE?!
!!!
TM-
TM-
TM-
TM-
TM-
TM-
TM-

NO WAY! THEY'RE ALL THE WAY OVER THERE?!
TM-TM-TM-TM-TM-

DARN IT! DON'T LET THEM GET AWAY, KARUDIO!
BOOM
PARU-PARU-MONN!
FWOOOOOMMMM

SHOOOOMM
A WALL MADE OF FLAME?!
WHY, HE...
HE'S CARRYING HIS PARTNER ON HIS BACK!

HOW COULD HE GET SO GOOD SO FAST?!
IT TOOK US SIX MONTHS TO GET TO THE LEVEL WE'RE AT NOW!
KARUDIO!
D- D-D- D- D D- D- D- D
CHASE THEM! CHASE THEM DOWN AND FINISH THEM...

KARUDIO?
...

I WAS AFRAID ....
I WAS AFRAID OF HIS EYES...
GLARE

THAT'S WHY I WAS TRICKED BY HIS FLAME, AND...
IN THE END ...

IN THE END...
I LET HIM GET AWAY ...

EVERY TIME HE STOOD UP, HE WAS CRYING OUT...
MERU...
...THE NAMES OF HIS PARTNER AND HIS MAMODO FRIENDS...
MERU...
RRG

...
OKAY, KARU-DIO.

I GUESS WE LOST THIS ONE.
BUT WE'LL GET THEM NEXT TIME.

THOSE TWO...
...ARE OURS.

LEVEL 176: Something Other than a Structure

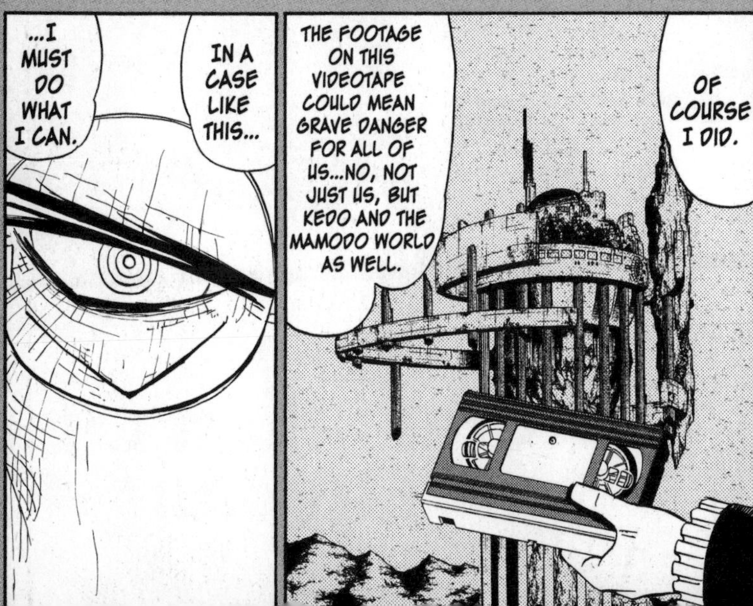

DR. RIDDLES!!!
LEVEL 176:
Something Other than a Structure

AND I BROUGHT MY LOVELY ASSISTANT, MISS SUSAN.
YAY!
BONK
TRIP

KIYO! ARE YOU OKAY?
OWWW
WH-WH-WHY DID YOU BRING MISS SUSAN?

WELL...
WHEN I TOLD HER I WAS GOING TO SEE KIYO, SHE ABSOLUTELY INSISTED ON COMING ALONG.

APPARENTLY, SHE WANTS TO SHOW YOU HER DANCE.
DANCE?!

ARE YOU READY?
YAY!

MUSIC START!
GACHA

CHA CHA CHA CHA

HEY, BIG BOY, WON'T YOU LOOK AT ME? ♡

CHA
CHA

CHA
CHA

IT'S OKAY, YOU CAN LOOK FOR FREE.

CHA
CHA
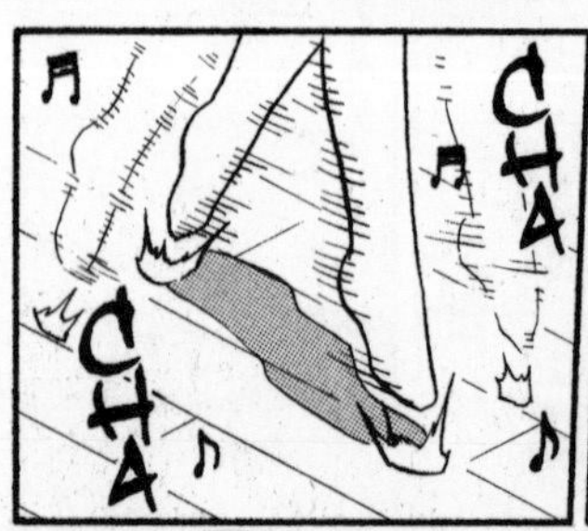
CHA
CHA

TAKE YOUR TIME, THERE'S NO NEED FOR HASTE. ♡
CHA CHA
CHA CHA

CHA CHA
CHA CHA
YOU DON'T WANT THIS TO GO TO WASTE!

CHA CHA
CHA CHA
CHA CHA
CHA CHA

SHOOBY DOOBY... SHOOBY DOOBY... SHOOBY DOOBY BA! ♡
CHA CHA

CHA CHA
SHOOBY DOOBY... SHOOBY DOOBY... SHOOBY DOOBY BA.

YAY!
CHA CHA
YAY!
GOOD!
CHA CHA

MY NAME'S MISS SUSAN AND I'M HERE TO STAY...
CHA CHA
CHA CHA

CHA CHA
CHA CHA

JUST DON'T CALL ME "SUSIE," OKAY? ♡
WINK

TA—DA

CLAP CLAP

CLAP CLAP CLAP

CLAP CLAP

ZAKER!
KABOOM
GYAAAAAAAAAAAA!

K-KIYO...
HOW COULD YOU DO THAT TO ME? HOW CRUEL...

BECAUSE YOU WERE SITTING THERE, WATCHING ME SUFFER, WITH A HUGE SMILE ON YOUR FACE.
UH...

WELL... IT WAS HILARIOUS... IT WAS SO PERFECT.
HEE HEE HEE... HO HO HO HO HO!

W-WAIT, I'M SORRY. I APOLOGIZE... WELL, LET ME GET TO THE POINT.
FWP...

AND THE POINT IS THE STRUCTURE THAT'S SHOWN IN THIS VIDEO-TAPE...
YEAH, DID YOU FIND OUT ANYTHING ABOUT IT?

ACTUALLY .... NOPE.
I COULDN'T FIND OUT A DARN THING!

GW
OO
ZAKER!
KABLAMM!

HUFF... HUFF... LOOK, PONY-GON!
WE FINALLY MADE IT HOME.
MERU-MERU~
HUH?

THE LIGHTS ARE ON IN MY ROOM...
AH!
I KNOW. IT MUST BE ZATCH AND KIYO.
KLAK
I GAVE HIM MY KEY BEFORE I LEFT FOR HOKKAIDO.

TA
DA

WHA-?
MERU ...
LONG TIME NO SEE, SUN-BEAM.
DR. RIDDLES AND EVERY-ONE... WHAT ARE YOU ALL DOING HERE?

WAIT, BEFORE THAT... DR. RIDDLES, WHY ARE YOU BURNT SO BADLY?
BECAUSE KIYO DIDN'T LISTEN TO WHAT I WAS SAYING.
I COULDN'T FIGURE OUT ANYTHING ABOUT THAT BUILDING FROM THE MAMODO WORLD, SO...
I THOUGHT WE COULD ALL POOL OUR MINDS AND THINK ABOUT IT.

I SENT OUT LETTERS TO EVERYONE SO THAT WE COULD COME TOGETHER IN A SPIRIT OF TEAMWORK... AND LOOK AT WHAT KIYO DID TO ME...
NAAW, I HAVE A FEELING THAT DR. RIDDLES GOT PUNISHED FOR TEASING KIYO...
SORRY FOR GOING IN YOUR ROOM WITHOUT PERMISSION.
I THOUGHT YOU WERE GOING TO COME HOME SOON.

NO, IT'S FINE.
I'M REALLY GLAD TO SEE YOU ALL.

WHAT HAPPENED TO YOU TWO? YOU LOOK HURT!
W-WELL, I'LL EXPLAIN THAT LATER.

SO, YOU WERE TALKING ABOUT THE BUILDING FROM THE MAMODO WORLD THAT WAS ON THE NEWS THE OTHER DAY?
YEAH, THAT'S RIGHT!

WHAT HAPPENED, ZATCH?
UH, WELL, WE JUST FOUGHT A MAMODO NAMED ARTH...

...AND HE SAID THAT THE BUILDING WAS THE "MENACE OF THE MAMODO WORLD."
YEAH, I'M PRETTY SURE THAT IT HAS SOMETHING TO DO WITH THE MAMODO WORLD.

WHAT BOTHERS ME IS SOMETHING THAT ARTH SAID.
HE SAID, "A STRUCTURE? THAT'S ALL IT APPEARS TO BE TO YOU?"

SO, THAT MEANS IT MUST BE SOMETHING OTHER THAN A STRUCTURE...
...BUT *WHAT?* THAT IS WHAT WE MUST DISCOVER!
DID YOU PUT IN THE TAPE, TIA?
YEAH, JUST PRESS PLAY.

I HAD NO IDEA IT WAS ON THE NEWS...
YEAH, WE DON'T HAVE A TV.
HEH HEH HEH... WE HAD NO IDEA ABOUT IT EITHER.
A BIG STAR HAS A BUSY SCHEDULE, SO...
OKAY, THERE IT IS! HIT PAUSE!
BEEP
WH—

WHOA! WHAT THE --?
WOW, THAT'S AMAZING!

IT'S SO HUGE...
JUDGING BY THE SIZE OF THE MOUNTAINS BELOW, THAT'S GOTTA BE ENOR-MOUS.

KANCHOMÉ, TIA, WONREI...DO YOU REMEMBER SEEING THIS IN THE MAMODO WORLD?
NO.

I RESEARCHED THIS FOOTAGE AS BEST I COULD.
HERE. TAKE A LOOK AT THESE CLOSE-UPS.

THESE THINGS ON THE TOP OF THE DOME ARE... HOUSES, RIGHT?
YEAH, THAT'S WHAT THE HOUSES IN THE MAMODO WORLD LOOK LIKE.

SO IT COULD BE A TOWN OF SOME KIND...
...

STARE

AH!

HUH? WHAT'S WRONG, KAN-CHOMÉ?
N-NO, IT'S NOTHING.
THAT CAN'T BE POSSI-BLE!
THAT CAN'T BE...
BA
"SOMETHING OTHER THAN A STRUCTURE ..."
...
STARE

YOU'RE ACTING STRANGE, KANCHOMÉ. IF YOU NOTICED SOMETHING, WE NEED YOU TO TELL US.
N-NO! IT'S NOTHING!

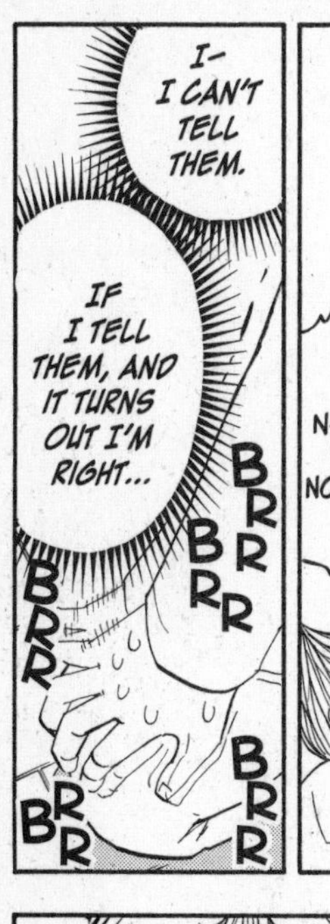
I- I CAN'T TELL THEM.
IF I TELL THEM, AND IT TURNS OUT I'M RIGHT...
BRR
BRR
BRR
BRR
BRR

IT MUST BE A MISTAKE. I DIDN'T REALLY SEE IT!
THAT'S RIGHT, IT'S JUST A MIS-TAKE!

BUT IF IT REALLY IS TRUE...
... THEN THAT WOULD MEAN ...

...THE END OF THE WORLD...

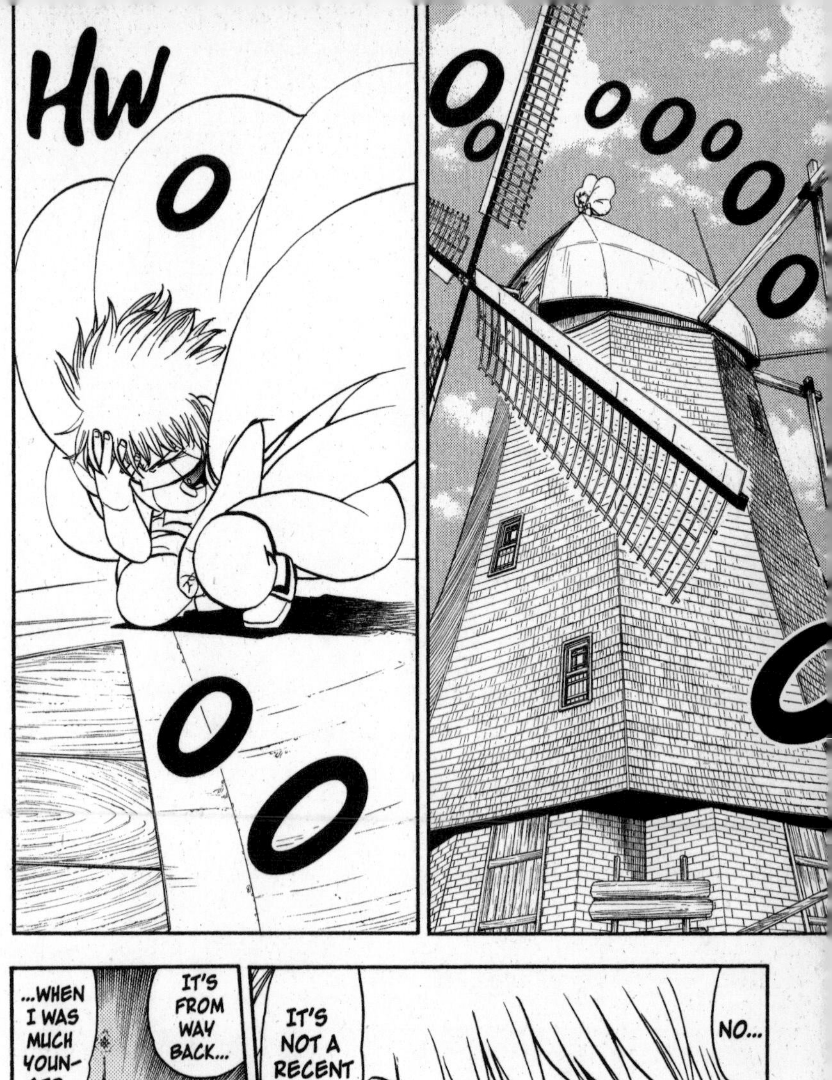
HWOOOOOOOOOOOO

NO...
IT'S NOT A RECENT MEMORY ...
IT'S FROM WAY BACK...
...WHEN I WAS MUCH YOUN-GER...

THAT'S RIGHT... IT WAS IN THE MAMODO WORLD...
IN THE KING'S LIBRARY...

I WENT INTO THE LABYRINTH AND...
BY ACCIDENT, I FOUND...

...THE FORBIDDEN BOOK-SHELVES.

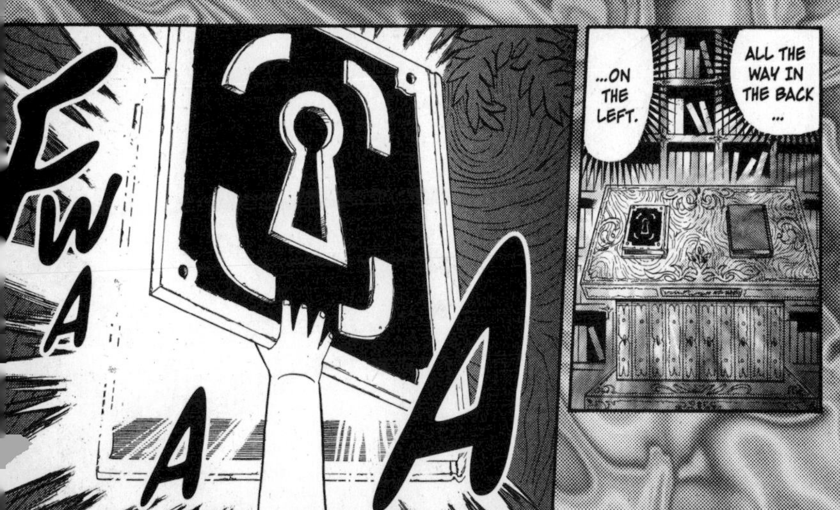
ALL THE WAY IN THE BACK ...
...ON THE LEFT.
FWAAAA

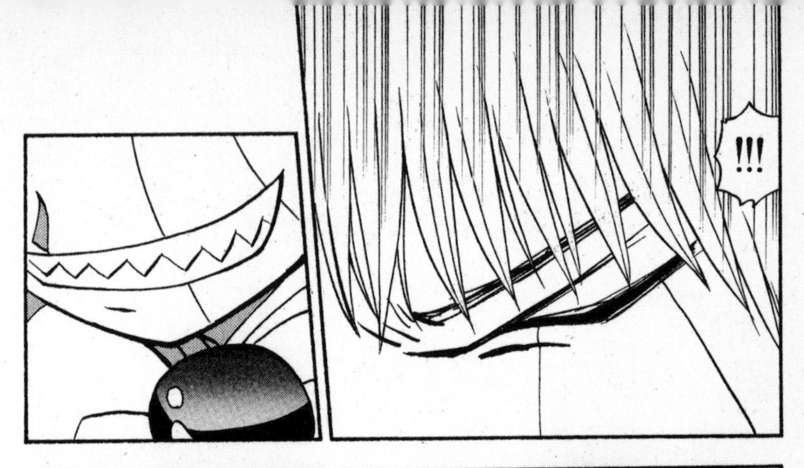
!!!

HOW AMUS-ING...
I DON'T KNOW WHO'S BEHIND THIS, BUT WHAT THEY'RE DOING IS VERY AMUSING INDEED.

BUT...
I'M NOT GOING TO LET THEM JUST DO WHATEVER THEY PLEASE.

FAUDO IS *MINE!*
AND *I'LL* BE THE ONE TO USE IT!

LEVEL 177: My Classmates

I COULDN'T DO ANYTHING TO HELP YOU AFTER ALL.
NO, IT WAS NICE TO SEE EVERYONE.

KIYO... MAY I ASK YOU ONE MORE THING?
HUH?
WHY DO YOU THINK THAT THE STRUCTURE FROM THE MAMODO WORLD DISAP-PEARED?
I THOUGHT OF SEVERAL POSSIBLE REASONS, BUT...
THE MOST LIKELY ONE IS THAT...

THEY WEREN'T FULLY PREPARED YET.

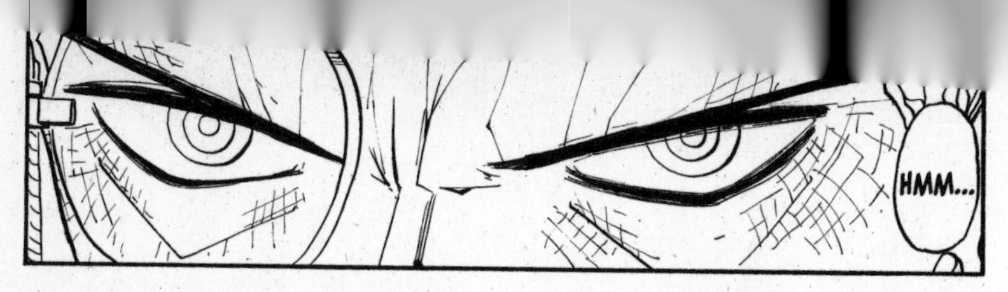
HMM...

SOME-BODY'S PLANNING ON DOING SOMETHING WITH THAT BUILDING, BUT...
...THEY'RE NOT PREPARED TO TAKE ACTION.
THAT'S WHY THEY MADE THE STRUCTURE APPEAR IN THE HUMAN WORLD...
...BUT AS SOON AS IT WAS DIS-COVERED, THEY MADE IT VANISH.

THEY DIDN'T WANT US TO ATTACK THE STRUC-TURE...
...BEFORE THEIR PLAN IS READY.
HMM... A VERY GOOD GUESS.

BUT JUST WHERE DID THE STRUCTURE DISAPPEAR TO?
I CAN'T ANSWER THAT YET.

I'M SURE THAT IT'S HIDDEN SOMEWHERE, BUT...
...I CAN'T IMAGINE THAT IT'S HIDDEN IN A LOCATION THAT CAN'T BE FOUND BY A SATELLITE CAMERA.

THE FACT THAT WE STILL CAN'T FIND IT MEANS...
IT MUST BE HIDDEN BY SOME KIND OF MAMODO SPELL.

ONLY A MAMODO...
...HAS THE ABILITY TO FIND IT.

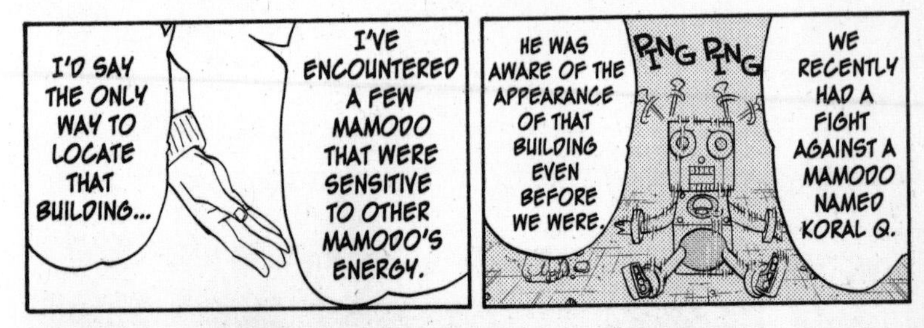
WE RECENTLY HAD A FIGHT AGAINST A MAMODO NAMED KORAL Q.
PING PING
HE WAS AWARE OF THE APPEARANCE OF THAT BUILDING EVEN BEFORE WE WERE.
I'VE ENCOUNTERED A FEW MAMODO THAT WERE SENSITIVE TO OTHER MAMODO'S ENERGY.
I'D SAY THE ONLY WAY TO LOCATE THAT BUILDING...

...IS TO FIND ONE OF THOSE "SENSITIVE MAMODO" OUT THERE.

YES.
I'M IM-PRESSED, KIYO.

KANCHOMÉ.
WH-WH-WHAT?

SH...

IF YOU EVER FIND THE COURAGE, TELL ME WHAT YOU NOTICED ABOUT THAT BUILDING.
OKAY?

WH-WHAT ARE YOU TALKING ABOUT, KIYO?
COME ON, LET'S GO, FOLGORE!
WE SHOULD BE GOING TOO...
AWW... I'LL MISS YOU.
IF YOU COULD'VE JUST WAITED FOR THREE MORE DAYS...
WE COULD'VE DONE SOMETHING CALLED "SKATING" TOGETHER.

SKATING?
YEAH, WE'RE GOING OUT WITH KIYO'S FRIENDS.

YEAH, IF WE ALL WENT OUT SKATING TOGETHER ...
I COULD INTRO-DUCE YOU TO MY CLASS-MATES.

I WISH I COULD GO...
MAYBE WE CAN STAY A LITTLE LONGER, LI-EN... I WANT TO BUY A TV ANYWAY...

WE CAN'T. IT'S ALMOST SPRING, SO WE'RE GONNA BE BUSY.
HA HA HA HA.

I HAVEN'T MET YOUR CLASS-MATES YET.
TELL ME, ZATCH! WHAT ARE KIYO'S CLASS-MATES LIKE?

WELL...
THEY'RE ALL FUN!
MERU-MERU-ME~
YEAH, THEY'RE ALL NICE PEOPLE.

I'M SURE THEY'LL GET ALONG WITH YOU ALL.
HA HA HA!
SKATE RINK
IT'S BEEN A LONG TIME SINCE THE LAST TIME I SKATED.

WHOA! LOOK, PONYGON! IT'S A HUGE BLOCK OF ICE.
ME, MERU-MERU.

HUH? WHY ARE YOU UPSET, PONYGON?
HA HA HA. PONYGON WAS ATTACKED BY A MAMODO WITH ICE POWERS.
YAY
WHZZ

OH, THAT'S RIGHT!
DON'T WORRY, PONYGON! THIS ICE IS SAFE.
YOU PLANNED THIS SKATING EVENT, RIGHT, SUZY?
ARE YOU A GOOD SKATER?
N-NO, I'M NOT THAT GOOD, BUT...
FLASHBACK
FLASHBACK

OH MY!
SLIP
OH NO! ARE YOU ALL RIGHT, MY DEAR?
OH, THANK YOU, JOHNNY!
CLASP
AHH, THIS IS IT!
THIS IS IT!
IF ONLY THAT COULD BE ME AND KIYO...
EEEK! TAKAMINE!
ARE YOU ALL RIGHT, MIZUNO?
SLIP
WOOSH
COME ON, HOLD MY HANDS...
ONE, TWO. ONE, TWO.
ONE, TWO. ONE, TWO.

OKAY, TAKAMINE! COME WITH ME! LET'S GO!
TMP
WHOA! HEY, WAIT...

KE R-WHAM
KYAAAAAA!

HA HA HA. WHAT'RE YOU DOING, SUZY?
OH, MARIKO ...

HEY, TAKAMINE. YOU CAN'T SKATE, HUH?
I'VE ONLY SKATED ONCE, BACK WHEN I WAS IN FIRST GRADE.

OH KIYO, THAT'S PATHE-TIC.
MERU-MERU-MEHA HA HA HA HA HA!
SHUT UP, ZATCH!
LET'S SEE *YOU* TRY IT!
SURE! YOU DON'T HAVE TO TELL ME TO. RIGHT, PONYGON?
MERU-MERU-ME~!
TMP

KER——WHAM
NGWAAAAAH!!!
MERUUUUUUUUU!

OWW... OWW...
MERU... RU RU RU RU...

LOOK AT YOU, ZATCH. YOU CAN'T SKATE!
SHAA
SHAA
WHY CAN'T I? EVERYONE ELSE MAKES IT LOOK SO EASY!

HA HA HA! WALKING AND SKATING ARE DIFFERENT BECAUSE YOU HAVE TO BALANCE DIFFERENTLY.
HE'S RIGHT. WE'LL SHOW YOU HOW TO SKATE!
CAN YOU SKATE, YAMA-NAKA?
OF COURSE I CAN. I MEAN, I'M AN AMAZING ATHLETE!
WHY WOULDN'T I BE ABLE TO SKATE?
YOU SAID IT!
GROOVY!
OE RENTAL
Shoes availab all size

WAP PA——WHAM
GYAAAAAAAAAAAAAAAAAAAAAAAAAAAAAAA!

W-WAAH... WHY? I'M SUPPOSED TO BE GOOD AT EVERY SPORT.
I EVEN RENTED A FIGURE SKATING UNIFORM...
THEY CAN'T SKATE EITHER...
I HATE ICE! I JUST HATE IT!
MERU.
BAMM
THEY SEEM TO BE UPSET ABOUT SOMETHING TOO...

HEH HEH HEH! WHAT THE HECK ARE YOU GUYS DOING? HOW EMBARRASS-ING.
YEAH, IT'S JUST SKATING!
LOOK HOW FABULOUS I AM, SUZY.
UH... HEY, SUZUKI. THAT'S SOME COSTUME YOU'VE GOT.
...
OKAY, LET'S GO!

KER-WHAM
GLAAAAAGGGGGGHHHHHHHHH!

WHY? WHY?! THE GREAT KANEYAMA CAN DO ANY-THING!
ROLL
BUT, WHEN THE UFO ABDUCTED ME, THEY GAVE ME THE PERFECT SKATER'S BODY...
ROLL

OH NO, MY COSTUME IS ALL TORN...
OKAY, WHO'S NEXT?

MY, MY. I'M DIS-APPOINTED, YOU GUYS.
ME TOO! I'LL SHOW YOU HOW TO SKATE.
I LEARNED THIS DANCE IN MOROCCO. IT'S CALLED THE WAKA MAKA DANCE.
WHAT? MOROCCO? WHEN DID YOU GO THERE?
STP
ARE YOU READY?
WAIT! WHAT'S THE WAKA MAKA DANCE?

WAKA MAKA MEKA MAKA MOO!
MOKO MAKA RAKA MAKA NAKA MAKA MAKE-KOO!
KA KA
KA KA KA
KA KA KA KA
KA
KA
WOW, HER DANCE MOVES ARE INCRED-IBLE!
SHE DIDN'T FALL!
THAT'S RIGHT. YOU HAVE TO USE YOUR HIPS WHEN YOU DO THIS DANCE!
YOU CAN'T JUST DANCE WITH YOUR FEET.

NYAGGGHH!!!
BAM
AGGGH! SABAE! SABAE!
GYAAAAH!
BANG
NOW EVERY-BODY HAS FALLEN DOWN...
YOU KNOW, I NEVER KNEW...
...THAT THE TEACHER'S WIFE'S NAME WAS SABAE...

WHAT'S WRONG WITH YOU GUYS? THIS IS NOTHING BUT A BLOCK OF ICE!
WHY CAN'T ANYBODY IN MY CLASS SKATE?

OH, I RUE THE DAY!
STUPID SKATING RINK!

FOR THE SAKE OF MY REPU-TATION...
I'LL MAKE EVERYONE IN MY CLASS LEARN TO SKATE!

HUH? NO...
I JUST WANT TO SKATE WITH TAKAMINE, THAT'S ALL...
THAT'S NOT GOOD E-NOUGH!
YOU THINK THAT'S MORE IMPORTANT THAN AVENGING SABAE'S HUMILI-ATION?
TM TM TM
UWAAAHHH!
SHWOOP

GA
CHANG

ALL RIGHT, PAY ATTENTION TO THIS FLAG!
TA-DAAA
WHOEVER GETS THIS FLAG FIRST IS THE WINNER!

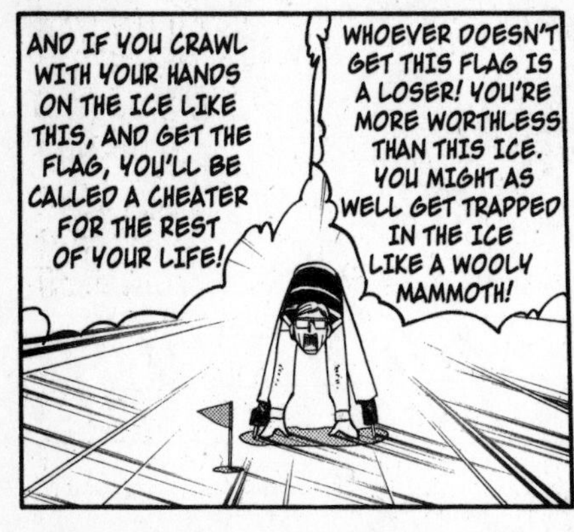
WHOEVER DOESN'T GET THIS FLAG IS A LOSER! YOU'RE MORE WORTHLESS THAN THIS ICE. YOU MIGHT AS WELL GET TRAPPED IN THE ICE LIKE A WOOLY MAMMOTH!
AND IF YOU CRAWL WITH YOUR HANDS ON THE ICE LIKE THIS, AND GET THE FLAG, YOU'LL BE CALLED A CHEATER FOR THE REST OF YOUR LIFE!

YEAH!
ALL RIGHT, ARE YOU READY?
ALL RIGHT, ON YOUR MARK.
GET SET...
GO!

A
A
A
A
A
GGGGGHHHHHHHHHHHHHHH!

SLAMMMMO
UNH... NGH...
FWIP
I'M NOT GONNA LOSE!
TM TM

SHWAPAPAP
YAAAAAAAAAAGGGGGG

GRAB
I WON'T LET YOU GO!
GYAAAA!
KA-BAM
Y-YOU GUYS...
DON'T BE SO SELFISH!
!!

KERWHAM
AGGGH!
MERU-MERU-ME~
BONK
SHWOOOP
T-TAKAMINE!
IWASHIMA!
...
KATUMP
KICKKICK
WAAAGYAAA
AHH...
THANK GOD...
I DIDN'T INTRODUCE MY FRIENDS TO WONREI AND LI-EN.
GYAAA
WAAAH
HYAA

LEVEL 178: A Letter for Zatch

HEY, KIYO! KIYO!
I GOT A LET-TER.

I GOT A LETTER ADDRESSED TO ME!
BANG
HUH?

IS IT FROM TIA OR KAN-CHOME?
WELL, ACTUALLY ...

I DON'T KNOW WHO IT'S FROM.

HMM... IT'S AIRMAIL.
PLEASE READ IT FOR ME, KIYO!
JAPAN

OKAY ...
"TO MY DEAR FRIEND ZATCH BELL."

WHOA, MY DEAR FRIEND? IT'S A LETTER FROM MY FRIEND?
HOP
HOP
"IT'S ME, REIN. LONG TIME NO SEE."

"REIN" ...DO YOU KNOW THIS GUY?
NO, I DON'T...

LET ME READ THE REST.
"I AM WRITING THIS LETTER TO ASK YOU TO DO ME A FAVOR."
"I WANT YOU ..."

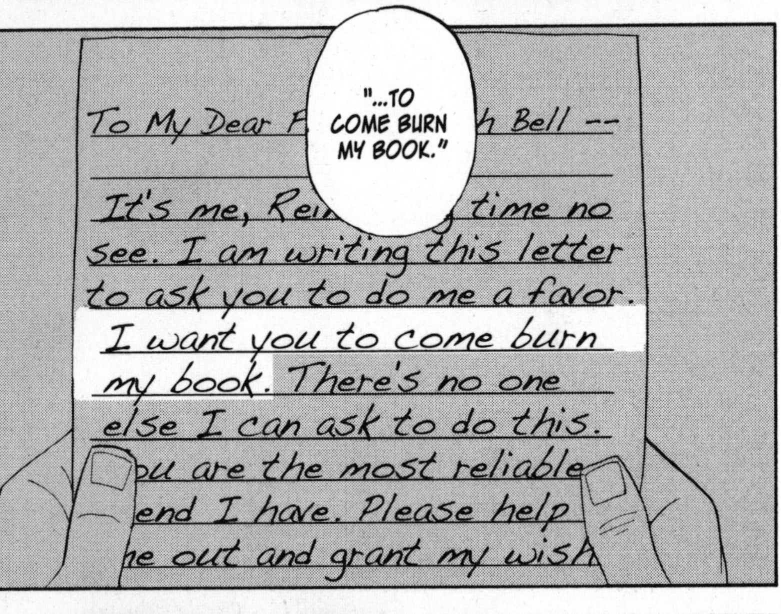
"...TO COME BURN MY BOOK."
To My Dear F h Bell --
It's me, Rei time no
see. I am writing this letter
to ask you to do me a favor.
I want you to come burn
my book. There's no one
else I can ask to do this.
ou are the most reliable
end I have. Please help
e out and grant my wish

WHA—?
...

GWO

GWO
"There's no one else I can ask to do this."

"You are the most reliable friend I have."
REIN

SHOOOOOOM
"Please help me out and grant my wish."
"I'll be waiting for you."
"Thanks for being my friend."

WOW, WHAT A BEAUTIFUL PLACE!
SHAA
WOW! I DIDN'T KNOW THERE WAS A COUNTRY LIKE THIS IN SOUTHEAST ASIA.

IT'S SMALL, BUT IT'S SURROUNDED BY NATURE. IT MUST BE NICE TO LIVE HERE.
KIYO! KIYO!

FLAP FLAP
LOOK AT THIS FISH! IT'S SO BIG AND COLORFUL!
WHAT THE HECK ARE YOU DOING NAKED ?!
FLAP FLAP
HEY, ZATCH...
IT SOUNDS LIKE THE LETTER WAS FROM SOMEONE YOU KNEW IN THE MAMODO WORLD...

BUT SINCE YOU DON'T REMEMBER ANYTHING ABOUT THE MAMODO WORLD...
WE CAN'T BE SURE THAT IT'S REALLY FROM YOUR FRIEND.
WHAT'RE YOU SAYING? I HAD A GOOD FRIEND IN THE MAMODO WORLD!
LOOK! IT SAYS, "YOU ARE THE MOST RELIABLE FRIEND I HAVE."

I HAVE TO GO HELP MY FRIEND!

TA
DA

WOW, WHAT A HUGE HOUSE!
THIS WOULD BE THE PERFECT PLACE TO AGREE TO MEET SOMEBODY NEXT TO.

OH, ARE WE MEETING HIM HERE?
NO, WE'RE SUPPOSED TO MEET FURTHER DOWN... BEHIND THE HOUSE...

I CAN'T WAIT TO MEET MY FRIEND... I WONDER WHAT HE'S LIKE...
TM TM TM TM
HEY, ZATCH. HAVE YOU FORGOTTEN WHAT HE ASKED YOU TO DO? HE ASKED YOU TO BURN HIS BOOK...THAT'S A SERIOUS REQUEST!

MI...

HUH?
MI...
MI...

A- ARE YOU REIN?
MI...

HOORAY! I WAS LOOKING FORWARD TO SEEING YOU! I'M YOUR BEST FRIEND, ZATCH BELL!
DASH
MI!

M-MIIII!
SHOOOP
YOU SCARED HIM AWAY, ZATCH.

NO, I DON'T THINK SO. HE'S JUST SHY.
TMTMTMTM
TM

RIGHT, REIN?
TMP
HE'S NOT REIN.

I AM.
ZATCH... HAVE YOU FOR-GOTTEN ME?

...
URK
WHOA!
OH...
SO YOU'RE MY BEST FRIEND, HUH?

OH, I SEE... YOU LOST YOUR MEMOR-IES...
YEAH, BUT THAT DOESN'T MEAN WE'RE NOT FRIENDS ANYMORE!
HA HA HA HA! DON'T WORRY ABOUT THAT!

EVEN THOUGH YOU LOST YOUR MEMOR-IES, YOUR PERSON-ALITY HASN'T CHANGED.
YOU'RE STILL THE SAME ZATCH.
THANKS FOR COMING.

OF COURSE! WE'RE BEST FRIENDS!
HA HA HA HA!
!!
OH! BY THE WAY, WHY DID YOU WRITE A LETTER...

...ASKING ME TO BURN YOUR BOOK?
REIN
OH, THAT'S ...
M-
MIIII!
KLATTER

HUH? WHAT'S WRONG?
SHIVER
SHIVER
SHIVER
SHIVER
M-MIIII!
I DON'T SEE ANYBODY ...
MIIIIII!

MIIIIIIIIIII!
DAA DUM

A FLY?
...
MIIII!
SIGH
IT'S NOT A BEE. IT DOESN'T HAVE A STINGER OR ANYTHING...
FWIP
FWIP
SMACK
GASP!

WHOAAAA!!!
...

FWIP
TURN
MI-MI-MIIII!
SHIVER SHIVER
SHIVER SHIVER

THIS IS...
...WHY I ASKED YOU TO BURN MY BOOK...

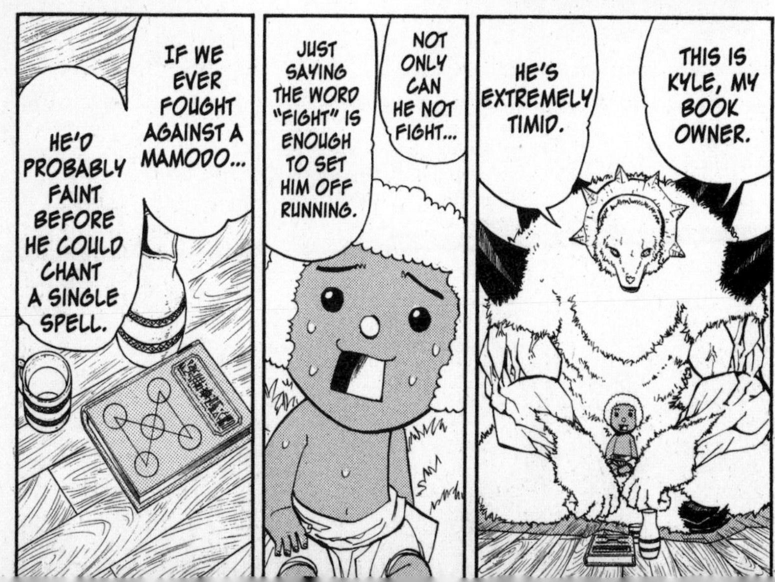
THIS IS KYLE, MY BOOK OWNER.
HE'S EXTREMELY TIMID.
NOT ONLY CAN HE NOT FIGHT...
JUST SAYING THE WORD "FIGHT" IS ENOUGH TO SET HIM OFF RUNNING.
IF WE EVER FOUGHT AGAINST A MAMODO...
HE'D PROBABLY FAINT BEFORE HE COULD CHANT A SINGLE SPELL.

HOW DID YOU MANAGE TO SURVIVE?
WE DON'T RUN INTO MAMODO OFTEN.
I'VE BEEN DEFEATING MAMODO BEHIND HIS BACK WITHOUT USING THE SPELLS.
PSST PSST
I SEE.
BUT FOR SOME REA-SON...

HE KEEPS LEARNING POWERFUL SPELLS...
WHAT?!

THE OTHER DAY, HE LEARNED A SPELL THAT WAS TOO POWERFUL.
I BLIND-FOLDED KYLE, AND HAD HIM CHANT THE SPELL...
FA SH
THE POWER WAS AMAZING!
IF KYLE SAW HOW POWERFUL THE SPELL WAS, HE'D PROBABLY DIE.
WELL, THAT'S NO GOOD.
I DON'T THINK I CAN TAKE THIS ANY LONGER...

KYLE ISN'T MENTALLY PREPARED FOR THE BATTLE OF THE MAMODO.
THAT'S WHY I WANT ZATCH TO BURN MY BOOK.
BOY, THAT'S A SHAME.
WHAT A WASTE... YOU'RE SO STRONG, AND YET YOU HAVE TO GIVE UP THE CHANCE OF BECOMING KING.
ACTUALLY... I DON'T REALLY CARE ABOUT BECOMING KING.
I'M ...
...MORE WORRIED ABOUT KYLE.
WOW, REIN. YOU SURE TAKE GOOD CARE OF HIM.

YES, WELL ...
HE SAVED MY LIFE.
WHAT? HOW?
M-
MIIIII!!!!!

WHAT NOW?
M-
M!!!!!
THAT'S ALL I HAVE FOR TODAY! I DON'T CARE IF YOU'VE GOT GUESTS!

SO NOW YOU'RE GOOD ENOUGH TO INVITE GUESTS, EH?
DO ON
M!!!!!
SHIVER SHIVER SHIVER
NOT AGAIN, JILL!
WHY DON'T YOU AT LEAST GIVE HIM ENOUGH FOR HIS GUESTS?
BA
MM

THE MONEY YOU HAVE BELONGS TO KYLE, DOESN'T IT?
!?
REIN ...?
TCH.

I'M TAKING CARE OF HIS FINANCES...
...BECAUSE THIS KID DOESN'T KNOW HOW TO HANDLE HIS MONEY, OKAY?
WHAT DO YOU KNOW, ANYWAY, REIN?
YOU'RE JUST A GUEST, AREN'T YOU? WHY DON'T YOU KEEP YOUR NOSE OUT OF THINGS THAT DON'T CONCERN YOU?

SO THAT'S IT...
HE CAN DISGUISE HIMSELF AS A HUMAN...
YOU'RE NOTHING BUT A TROUBLE-MAKER. NOW GET OUT OF HERE!
YOU BIG OAF!
GRAB

FINE! TAKE IT!
M-
M-----!
WP
WP
RRG...
COME ON, KYLE.
M------!
TP
TP
TP
...
SIGH...

KYLE'S THE SON OF THE MAYOR OF THIS TOWN. WHEN HIS FATHER PASSED AWAY...
KYLE INHERITED LOTS OF MONEY, BUT...

THE PEOPLE WHO MANAGE HIS MONEY ARE TAKING ADVANTAGE OF HIM.
IF KYLE WAS ABLE TO SPEAK UP, HE COULD FIRE THEM, BUT...
YEAH, KYLE NEEDS TO BE STRONGER.
EVEN IF YOU HELP HIM OUT ONCE OR TWICE, PEOPLE LIKE THAT WILL KEEP COMING BACK.

HE NEEDS TO LEARN TO SPEAK UP FOR HIMSELF.
YEAH, AND...
SOMEDAY REIN MIGHT HAVE TO GO BACK TO THE MAMODO WORLD. MAYBE...MAYBE SOMETIME SOON!
MI?
MII! MII!
I'M JUST WORRIED ABOUT LEAVING HIM BEHIND.

BUT I HAVE NO OTHER CHOICE.
IT'S BETTER THAN SEEING KYLE GET HURT IF WE'RE ATTACKED BY OTHER MAMODO...
OKAY, KYLE. LET'S FORGET ABOUT BURNING REIN'S BOOK, AND...
...FIGHT AGAINST THE MAMODO TOGETHER!
SHIVER
SHIVER
SHIVER
SHIVER
M-MI MI MI MI MI MI...

IF KYLE ONLY HAD COURAGE...
I KNOW HE'S GOT STRENGTH DEEP INSIDE HIM...
WHERE IS IT?! WHERE DID THE MONSTER GO?!
I DON'T KNOW! HE'S GONE. I THOUGHT IT WAS TOO INJURED TO MOVE...!

...
SKF... SKF...
HUFF...
HUFF...
HUFF...

HUFF...
SKFFFF...
SKFFF...
SKF...
HUFF...

LEVEL 179: That Person

HMM.
BEFORE WE BURN REIN'S BOOK, LET'S SEE WHAT WE CAN DO ABOUT KYLE'S SITUATION.
YEAH! GOOD IDEA, KIYO!
SWING

KYLE'S REAL HOUSE IS OVER THERE...
IT'S SO WRONG THAT HE CAN'T EVEN LIVE THERE.
KYLE'S REAL HOUSE
THE PLACE WHERE KYLE LIVES

REALLY?
WILL YOU HELP ME?
OF COURSE! WE CAN'T SEND YOU BACK TO THE MAMODO WORLD...
...BEFORE YOU MAKE SURE THAT KYLE IS ALL RIGHT.
HE'S RIGHT, KYLE. LET'S HANG IN THERE!
MII!

THANK YOU.
I'M SO GLAD THAT I ASKED ZATCH TO COME...

ALL RIGHT THEN, LET'S GET STARTED RIGHT AWAY.
?

YOU'RE REALLY IN A HURRY, HUH?
AH, YEAH...

SOME STRANGE MAMODO CAME BY RECENTLY, ASKING US TO JOIN THEIR GROUP.
IF WE RUN INTO THEM AGAIN, IT COULD BE TROUBLE.

THEY ASKED YOU GUYS TO JOIN THEM?
YES, THEY SAID THEY WANTED OUR HELP...
I SEE...
JUST AS I SUSPECTED... THERE'S SOMEONE ELSE BUILDING AN ARMY OF MAMODO...
WHAT KIND OF MAMODO COULD THEY BE?

GAAAANGS OF...
...NEWWW YOOORK!!!

WHAT ON EARTH ARE YOU SINGING ABOUT, POORY?
EVIL. I'M SINGING ABOUT *EVIL*, LUPA.

OH, SO YOU GREW THAT MUSTACHE TO LOOK EVIL, HUH?
EH, POORY?

...
WHO'S "POORY"? MY NAME IS PURIO, YOU KNOW.

"POORY" IS SHORT FOR PURIO.
POORY, POORY,
POORY!!

...
I GUESS IT'S NOT BAD.
YES, IT'S NICE, ISN'T IT?

BY THE WAY, WHAT ARE WE GOING TO DO WITH THAT REIN MAMODO?
HE DOESN'T SEEM INTER-ESTED IN JOINING US.

WELL, IN THAT CASE, WE'LL JUST HAVE TO TAKE EXTREME MEASURES...
!!

WAIT, LUPA, THEY'RE COMING OUT NOW.

OH! WHO ARE *THESE* PEOPLE?
THEY'VE GOT TWO STRAN-GERS WITH THEM...

AH-AWAGGGH!
IT'S *THEM!*

ALL RIGHT, KYLE, ARE YOU READY?
JUST IMAGINE THAT KIYO IS JILL, AND SAY IT OUT LOUD!!

"I HATE YOU, JILL! I WANT YOU TO GET OUT OF MY HOUSE!"
LIKE THAT.

COME ON, KYLE. DON'T BE SHY!
MII...

I H-HATE Y-YOU...
J-JILL... M-MII-MII-MIIIIII...
B- B- BMP BMP

YOU CAN SAY IT, KYLE!
MII... M-MI-MII-MIIII-IIII...
B- B- BMP BMP

JYAAAAAAAAAAAAAAAHHHHHHHH!!!
KOAK
MIIIIIIIIIIIIIIIIIII!!!

KYLE...
M-M-MII-MII-MIIIII-III!!!
ZOOM

IMAGINATION
EXCUSE ME, JILL. IS IT TRUE THAT YOU'RE MISTREATING THIS BOY?
IMAGINATION
EVEN IF HE FINDS AN ADULT WHO WILL STAND UP FOR HIM...

YOU'RE RIGHT ...
HMM... THIS ISN'T GOOD. HE CAN'T EVEN SAY IT TO ME.

M-M-MII-M------...
IF YOU EVER BRING THOSE GUYS HERE AGAIN, I AM GOING TO BEAT YOU SENSELESS!!!

M... M-MII-MII-MIIIIII...
I AM NOT MIS-TREATING YOU, AM I, KYLE?

YEAH ...
NO ONE CAN HELP HIM WHILE HE'S LIKE THAT.

STILL, KYLE NEEDS TO BE ABLE TO TALK TO THE PEOPLE WHO CAN HELP HIM.
WE MIGHT BE ABLE TO GET JILL FIRED IF WE CAN GATHER ENOUGH PROOF OF HER WRONG-DOINGS...
ZONY

YES ... HMM ...
STUFF LIKE THAT MIGHT HAPPEN.

REMEMBER, YOU HAVEN'T DONE ANYTHING WRONG!
SO YOU SHOULDN'T BE SCARED! JILL'S THE ONE WHO SHOULD BE SCARED! BE BRAVE!

MII...
GLOOOM
M.........

MII...
...

I THOUGHT...

ZATCH COULD HELP HIM SOMEHOW, BUT...

I HAVE NO CHOICE.
WE HAVE TO BURN THE BOOK...
MII...
MII MII...
TMP

M---!!
GRAB

WHAT?! KYLE!!
TM TM TM TM TM
M---!!

WAIT, THE BOOK...!
TM TM TM TM TM

NOW'S OUR CHANCE! LET'S GET HIM!
TMTM
!!!

I WON'T LET YOU BURN YOUR BOOK!!!
M---!!!!
GRAB
TUMBLE

LISTEN TO YOURSELF. YOU'RE GOING TO BURN YOUR OWN BOOK? FORGET IT!
THAT'S RIGHT, REIN! INSTEAD, YOU'RE GOING TO JOIN OUR TEAM!
SHAAAAAA

WHA—?!

HUH?

PANBURI... AND MOJAMOJA...
YOU TWO ARE STILL ALIVE?
YOU GOT OUR NAMES WRONG, ZATCH! MY NAME IS *PURIO!*

HMPH! I DON'T CARE HOW MUCH WE NEED PEOPLE IN OUR TEAM...
WE DON'T NEED *YOU* IDIOTS!
WHAT WE WANT IS REIN'S POWER!
POINT

REIN, THIS KID IS NOW OUR HOSTAGE!
IF YOU WANT TO SAVE HIM, YOU HAVE TO JOIN OUR TEAM...
RAAAAAAHHHHHH!!!
EH?

DON'T YOU HURT KYLE!
DM DM
UWAAAH! THIS IS NONE OF YOUR BUSINESS!
DWAAAA

CURSES! TIME FOR A STRATEGIC WITHDRAWAL!
REIN, WHEN YOU'RE READY TO JOIN US, COME TO THE WEST SIDE OF THE COAST AT NIGHTFALL...
ZSSSHH
NUOOOOOOO!!!
GYAAAGGH
I SAID, DON'T FOLLOW US!!!

ZOOOOM
WAAAAAAAAAAAAAAAAAAAAAAAAAAAAAAAAAAAHHHHHHHHHHHHHHHHHHHHHHHHH

LOOK, WE ENDED UP COMING ALL THE WAY TO OUR MEETING PLACE!!
G... GIVE... KYLE... BACK...

DAREIDO!!
LUPA, TIME TO USE THE GLUE!
FWA

BLARF

SPLAT
DAAAAAAHHHHHHHH!!!!
HYOOOO
M----!!!

SPLAPP

YES! WE'VE GOT HIM.
NOW WE'RE READY TO FIGHT, ZATCH! ARE *YOU?*
I'VE BECOME A BAD GUY, YOU KNOW!!
I'LL SHOW YOU HOW STRONG I'VE BECOME!!

GI-GANO JOBO-IDO!!
FOOSHHHHHH

HA HA HA! DO YOU SEE THAT? THIS LIQUID IS STRONG ENOUGH TO MELT ROCKS!
FSSSSH

ALL OF YOU WILL SIZZLE AND MELT!

ZAGURZEM!
BAYOOO
ZAKERUGA!!
FASH

DGOOON

DSSHHHH
...
...
SHIVER SHIVER SHIVER SHIVER
SHIVER
SHIVER

OOOOOOOO

HYOOOOO

M-
MOKERUDO!!
BLEAHH

W-WHAT SHOULD WE DO, LUPA? OUR MOST POWERFUL SPELL DIDN'T WORK!
THOSE GUYS HAVE GOTTEN STRONGER TOO!

NONE OF OUR OTHER SPELLS WORK VERY WELL. I DON'T THINK WE CAN DEFEAT THEM.
ALL WE HAVE ARE A BUNCH OF USELESS SPELLS.

ZAKER!!
AIEEE!!!
BAS HOOM

TH-THEY WERE ABLE TO AIM AT US BY JUST LISTENING TO THE SOUND OF OUR VOICES!
UH-OH... THEY REALLY ARE BETTER THAN US...

LET'S GET OUT OF HERE!
SOUNDS GOOD TO ME!

AHH, BUT...!
WE CAN'T JUST RUN AWAY LIKE THIS! IF WE DO...

BOOOM
AAAAAHHHHH!!
HOW DID HE GET UP THERE?

MII ...
DON'T WORRY, KYLE. I'LL SAVE YOU.

AAHHHH!! WHAT SHOULD WE DO? WHAT SHOULD WE DO?
WE CAN'T GET REIN TO JOIN OUR TEAM AND WE CAN'T DEFEAT ZATCH!!

IF WE RUN AWAY NOW...
WE'LL BE KILLED BY... HIM!
SHIVER
OKAY ...
I'VE GOT YOU...
HA!!
AGGGGH!
KICK

PURIO.
WHY IS IT TAKING YOU SO LONG TO GET THIS MAMODO TO JOIN US?

WAH!
LORD RO-DEAUX!
!!
NGH ...

LEVEL 180: Meeting in the Mamodo World

WHO ARE THEY...?

L-L-LORD RODEAUX! PLEASE FORGIVE US...
WE WERE SO CLOSE TO GETTING REIN ON OUR TEAM.

WHAT ARE YOU TALKING ABOUT?
I WAS WATCHING YOU. YOU WERE JUST ABOUT TO RUN AWAY, WEREN'T YOU?

N-NO!
WE'D NEVER DO THAT!!
REIN !!
!!
WE COULD USE POWER LIKE YOURS.
WHY DON'T YOU JUST STOP THIS FIGHTING, LISTEN TO MY OFFER AND JOIN US?
HMPH... SO IT WAS YOU WHO SENT THESE FOOLS.
WELL, TOO BAD.

I'VE DECIDED TO BURN MY BOOK...
...AND WITHDRAW FROM THE BATTLE.
...

HMPH...
THAT'S NO FUN.
YOU HAVE THE POWER TO WIN, BUT DON'T WANT TO USE IT.
YOU'RE A FOOL...
IN FACT...
YOU MAKE ME SICK...

DIOGA RAGYUR!!

R...
...RAUZARUK!
FASH
NRAAAAHHH!
DOOM
FWIP
AGGGGGGHHHHHH!
DGOOOM

ULP...
WHAT A PSYCHO... USING SUCH A POWERFUL SPELL WITHOUT WARNING...
GWOOOO
SO...
...

YOU HAD TO BUTT IN...

HEY, BOY. IF YOU JUST GO HOME QUIETLY AND DON'T BOTHER US AGAIN, I'LL LET YOU OFF THE HOOK THIS TIME.

AND RUN OUT ON A FRIEND ...?

HOW BOR-ING ...

THERE'S NOTHING MORE FUN THAN SHOOTING SOME FOOL IN THE BACK...
...AS HE RUNS AWAY, LEAVING HIS FRIEND BEHIND.
SNEER

WHY YOU...

ZATCH!!
RRAAAHHHHH!!!
WOOM
!!!
HYOO
FWIP

NRAAAAHH!!!
KRASH

HMPH... YOUR PHYSICAL STRENGTH HAS BEEN ENHANCED...
BUT...
IT WON'T BE ENOUGH!
FWAP

GANZU RAGYUR!!
KYUKYU
KYU
KYU
KYU
KYU
KYU
KYU
KYOON

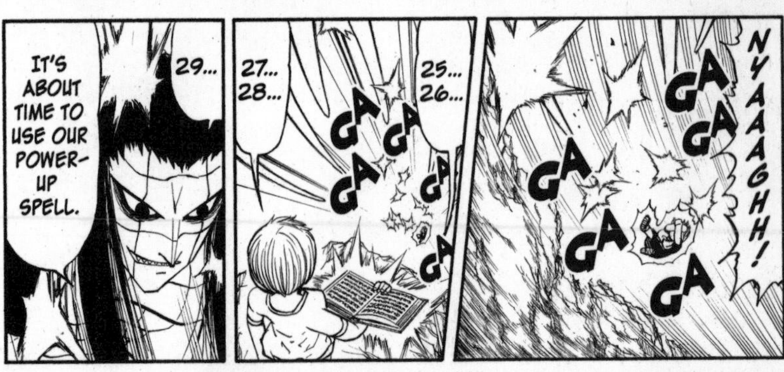
NYAAAAGHH!
GA GA GA GA GA GA
25... 26...
27... 28...
GA GA GA GA GA GA
29...
IT'S ABOUT TIME TO USE OUR POWER-UP SPELL.

HUH?
FWSH
RAUZARUK IS....
TMP
HAH!
ZAM
!!?

RA-GYURU ROSU-DO!!
DOKOM
GAAAAAAAAAH!!!

THEY CAUGHT US OFF GUARD WHEN THE RAUZARUK SPELL WAS FADING!!
ZATCH!!

CHITA, WHY DIDN'T YOU CAST THE OTHER SPELL, DIORUGA RAGYUR?
WE DON'T HAVE ENOUGH STRENGTH FROM WITHIN!
THERE'S NO WAY THAT WE CAN USE SUCH BIG SPELL OVER AND OVER.

OH NO...
THEY'RE ON A DIFFERENT LEVEL. ZATCH CAN'T...
ZATCH, DON'T EVEN TRY TO GO AFTER HIM WHEN HE'S FLYING!
IF YOU ATTACK HIS PARTNER, HE'LL HAVE TO COME DOWN TO THE GROUND TO DEFEND HER!
RRAHHHH!
TOOM

HMPH. ABSURD.
THOSE KINDS OF TACTICS WON'T WORK ON ME.
TM TM TM
PURIO!!
NYUREIDO!!
BLEAGX

SLIP
SLIP
P P P
NWAAAAAH!

AHH, I CAN'T GET UP, IT'S TOO SLIPPERY...
SLIP
SPLASH
MOSREIDO!!
SPLRSSS
H H

SHWAA A A
HUH?
FOG?
!!
PLUMP
PLUMP

OWWWWWW!
SCRCH
SCRCH
SCRCH
SCRCH
IT'S SO ITCHY! MY WHOLE BODY ITCHES!!

IT WORKED!! MY USELESS SPELL IS ACTUALLY WORKING ON HIM!!
THIS IS GREAT, POORY!

HANG IN THERE...
IF WE CAN JUST NAIL THE PARTNER...
NHH...
SCRITCH
NHH...
SCRATCH
HE'S NOT LISTENING TO ME!
THE INTENSE ITCHING IS MAKING HIM LOSE HIS CONCENTRATION!!

HA HA HA!
GIGANO RAGYUR!!
NGH ...
AHHHHHHHHHH!
BA
M
M
GASHOOM
NRAAAHH!
M

GRR...
YOU LITTLE PEST!
AGGHH!
WH
AK
THIS LITTLE BRAT ...
...CAN HARDLY EVEN OPEN HIS EYES, AND YET HE ATTACKS ME?
SKID

WH- WHERE ARE YOU?!
I'LL KILL YOU IF YOU HURT KIYO OR REIN AND KYLE!!

BAM
THAT'S RIGHT.
NOW I RE-MEM-BER...

I SAW THIS ONCE BEFORE...
ARGGGHHH!
NRRGH...HOW COULD I HAVE DONE THIS TO MYSELF? I SLIPPED AND FELL ALL THE WAY DOWN TO THE BOTTOM OF A CLIFF...
!!
STAB
B

GRAGGGGGHHHHHHHH!
OH NO...
IF I MOVE EVEN THE SLIGHTEST, I FEEL THIS SHARP, STABBING PAIN...
...AND I CAN HARDLY BRE-ATHE...
GGH...
NHH...
GLGH...
BLRGH!
I HAVE TO GET HELP...
...FROM THE VILLAGERS UP ABOVE...
...
BUT... WHO WOULD COME AND HELP ME?
"REIN IS ON A RAMPAGE AGAIN!!"
"NOBODY CAN STOP HIM NOW!!"
"HOW MANY PEOPLE DID HE HURT THIS TIME?"
"WILL SOMEONE PLEASE JUST GET RID OF HIM... PLEASE..."
THIS IS...
...THE END FOR ME...

HEY, ARE YOU ALL RIGHT?
!!
QUICK, LET ME HELP YOU! ALL THAT BLOOD...
RG
SH-SHUT UP!!
RRGG
FOOL! DON'T YOU KNOW WHO I AM?
ANYBODY WHO MESSES WITH ME WILL BE RIPPED INTO PIECES BY MY CLAWS!!
YOU DARE APPROACH ME, YOU LITTLE BRAT?
IF YOU DON'T LEAVE RIGHT NOW...
WSH
BLRGH
NGH...
I'LL RIP YOUR GUTS OUT!

WHAT ARE YOU TALKING ABOUT? YOU'RE THE ONE WHO'S ALREADY RIPPED APART!
IF YOU DON'T LET ME HELP YOU, YOU'RE GONNA DIE!!
WHEN ZATCH SAID THAT, SUDDENLY EVERYTHING CHANGED FOR ME...
HE TAUGHT ME THE TRUE MEANING OF STRENGTH...
EVEN WHEN I WAS MAD WITH POWER...
...HE STOOD UP TO ME.
WHAT WAS I THINKING?
I SHOULDN'T BE ASKING ZATCH TO CURE KYLE'S COWARDICE...

ZU
GIGANO RAGYUR !!
HA HA HA YOU'VE LEFT YOUR PARTNER ALL ALONE!
AA
GWO O
UH-OH...
KIYO !!

KRRKKAOOOOOM

HyOooo oo
I HAVE TO...

GRRRR
I HAVE TO HELP KYLE MYSELF...

HMPH ...
MII...

KYLE...
WATCH ME REAL CLOSE...
BE-CAUSE THIS MAY BE...

...THE LAST TIME YOU'LL EVER SEE ME!!
GRAAAAAAAAAAAAAHHHHHHHHHHHHH!!!!
LEVEL 181: A Scary Appearance

GRAAAAAAAAAAAAAAAAAHHHHHHHHHHHHHHHHHHH
WOW ...
WHAT ...
HA HA HA.
NOW THAT'S MORE LIKE IT!

HA!!
DOOM

UGAAH!
!!
DASH

HUH?!

CHIITA, THE SPELL...

NOPE. I CAN'T ...
HE'S GOT US.

GRAAAAAAAHHHHHH!!!!!
GWOHHHHHHHH!!

KA SHOOOOOM

EEK!
FWAAA

WHOA ...
HE DIDN'T EVEN USE A SPELL...

SPLAS
GRR...
HA
URAAAAHH!

CHIITA, WHY DIDN'T YOU USE A SPELL TO COUNTER HIM?!
BECAUSE I KNEW I COULDN'T DO IT ON TIME. WE CAN'T EXPEND OUR SPELLS RECKLESSLY.

WE'VE USED QUITE A FEW SPELLS AL-READY.
WE HAVE TO PACE OUR SPELL USE APPROPRIATELY, OTHERWISE WE CAN'T WIN.

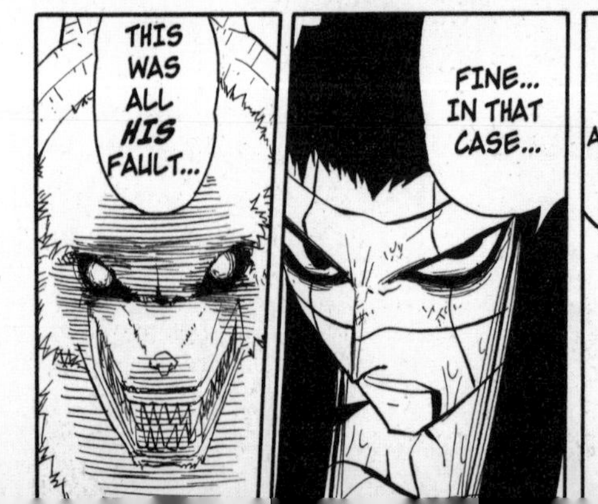
FINE... IN THAT CASE...
THIS WAS ALL HIS FAULT...

DON'T MESS WITH ME, YOU SCUM!
URAAAAAHH!
GAH

KNG
TNG
KLANG
MII... SHIVER MII...
SHIVER
...
NOW WE'VE GOT HIM.

GIGANO RAGYUR !!

GYAAAAAHH!!
ZZZYYAAA
HMPH.
YOU BLOCKED IT WITH YOUR OWN BODY AGAIN, EH?
GAOOOOO

GWAAAA
BAM
KRASH
M-------!!!!

HNNNNN
HNNN
HNNNNNNNN
MII...
MII-
MII...

GROOOOOOHHHHHH!
MII——!!
GRAHHHHHHHHH!

KRAKABOOOMMM

THUD
MII...
MII...
...
DO I SCARE YOU, KYLE?

SHIVER SHIVER
MII...
SHIVER
SHIVER
I KNOW YOU'RE SCARED.
BUT YOU KNOW WHAT?

WHEN SOMEBODY GETS REALLY SERIOUS, THEY LOOK SCARY.
ESPECIALLY WHEN THEY'RE TRYING TO PROTECT SOMEBODY THEY LOVE.

MI...
MI...
I DON'T KNOW HOW I LOOK TO YOU...
...IF I LOOK GOOD OR EVIL...

BUT...
I HAVE TO DO THIS.

M------!!
SMASH

SHIVER
SHIVER
SHIVER
SHIVER
SHIVER SHIVER

HMPH...
BRR
BRR
BRR
BRR BRR BRR
I CAN'T TEACH YOU LIKE ZATCH CAN...

SHF

WHAT A FOUL CREATURE I AM.
I CAN ONLY PROTECT YOU LIKE THIS.

MII...
AHA, THERE YOU ARE!!
KYOON
KYU
KYU
KYU
KYU KYU
GANZU RAGYUR!!

URAAHHHHHHH!!!
D D D D D D D D D

WHAT ARE YOU DOING?!
D D
GET OUT OF HERE, NOW!!
MII...
TMP...
M------!!!
M------!!!
TM TM TM TM TM
...

KYLE, I KNOW THAT YOU'LL BE STRONG LIKE ZATCH SOMEDAY...
YOU TWO ARE VERY MUCH ALIKE.

YOU'LL BE ABLE TO STAND UP TO ANYONE.
SKR

ANY-ONE ...
...IN THE WHOLE WIDE WORLD ...

GR
AB
GRAAAAH!
WOOSH
HMPH!
WHAT A PEST!
KRASSHH

YWA
YAAAAAAAH!
!!!
ZAGURZEM!
HUH?!
BA
GYOOM

GRR...
WHAT IS THIS SPELL...?
GWOOOO

C'MON ZATCH! ONE MORE TIME!
TM
TCH!

NOT SO FAST!
AMIREIDO!!
VASHEENG
GWAAAAAAAAHHHHHH!

HA HA HA HA HA!
WAAHH!!
TMTMTMTMTM

EAT SAND, FOOLS!!
TOSS
TOSS
HEH HEH HEH! HERE COME THE CRABS. THEY'RE GONNA PINCH YOUR BUTTS!
PINCH PINCH

URGGHH
RRGGH!!
HA HA, DON'T EVEN TRY. YOU'VE GOT TO HAVE SOME REAL STRENGTH TO BREAK THROUGH THAT NET...

HERE GOES, POORY. LET'S FINISH THEM OFF!
NO, WAIT. LET'S TEASE THEM SOME MORE...

ROARRRRRRRRRRR!!!
THMAW
GYAAAAAAAAAAAAAH!

REIN!
STUPID NET...
RRRGG

HOW DARE YOU!
GIGANO JYO-BOIDO!!
SPEW
GAAHH...
WWWW

URAAAAAAAAAAHHHHHHHH!

REIN!
FSSSSSS
GH...
GYAAAAAAAAH!
OHHHHH!
SHIVER
SHIVER
GET OUT OF MY WAY!
WOOSH
YEEEEEEEK!!
"I DON'T KNOW HOW I LOOK TO YOU..."
SHIVER
SHIVER
"IF I LOOK EVIL..."
"...OR GOOD..."

"BUT I HAVE TO DO THIS!!"

...

WHAT DO YOU THINK, CHIITA? DO YOU THINK YOU CAN USE OUR MOST POWERFUL SPELL NOW?
YES, I'M READY...
FASH
WHAT ...?

NO WAY... DO THEY STILL HAVE ENOUGH STRENGTH FROM WITHIN?
THEY WERE TALKING ABOUT PACING THEIR SPELLS... ARE THEY REALLY THAT POWERFUL?

ZATCH, FORGET ABOUT THE NET! WE'RE IN A TIGHT SPOT, BUT TURN YOUR HEAD TOWARDS THE ENEMY!
LET'S TRY ONE MORE ZAGURZEM...

!!!
WHAT?
OOOOOO
WHO'S THAT?
WHAT IS THAT STRENGTH FROM WITHIN?

GAWOOOOOO

LEVEL 182: It's Okay Now

ZA
GOGOMMM
LEVEL 182:
It's Okay Now

HWOOOOOOOOOOO

MII, M-M-MI-MII-MIIIIIIII!!
SHIVER
SHIVER
SHIVER
SHIVER
YOU LITTLE—
CAN'T LET DOWN MY GUARD!!
LEAP

OH NO. THEY'RE GOING FOR KYLE, AND THEY'RE CLOSER!
RRAHHH!
DOOOM
OH NO.
IT'S TOO LATE...

ZAGURZEM!
WHOOPS!
BOOM
BASH
FOOLS! YOU MISSED!!
YOU THOUGHT YOU'D HIT ME FROM BEHIND, BUT...
ZZZT

ZAKERUGA!!
GYOOOMMM

HA! YOU THINK YOU CAN GET ME WITH THA...
FWOO
BOOM
!!?
KA-BOOM

GWAAAAAAAAAHHHHHHHHH!!
KA-BLAM
NNH ...
WHA ...?
WHAT POWER... THAT SPELL ZAGURZEM STORES UP ELECTRICAL POWER.
ON TOP OF THAT, IT CAN CAUSE A CHAIN REAC-TION.
ZZT
ZZT
ZZT
ZZT

KYLE!!
MII!!

RRG
RRG
RRG
RRG
GH... GGHH ...
RRG

WHAT THE HECK ARE YOU DOING?!
VOOM

KEEP YOUR EYES ON HIM, ZATCH!
GYOOO
WHAT SHOULD I DO? SHOULD I USE ZAGURZEM OR BAO ZAKERUGA?

THERE'S NO POINT IN LAUNCHING ANOTHER SHOT.
IT DOESN'T MATTER WHAT SPELL YOU USE. IT WON'T HIT RODEAUX WHILE HE'S MOVING.

ONCE WE'RE IN CLOSE ...
...WE'LL BLAST YOU TO PIECES.

REIN! COME ON!
!!?

SHIVER
I GOTTA HELP ZATCH!!
SHIVER
SHIVER
SHIVER
SHIVER
SHIVER
HA HA HA!
VERY GOOD!
LET'S ...
... SAVE HIM TOGE-THER!!
BOOM

WSH
WSH
WHS
ARGH... HE'S TOO FAST...
C'MON!
HURRY!
...

SHIVER
SHIVER
SHIVER
HE'S TRYING TO STAY STRONG, BUT HE'S PUSHED TO THE LIMIT...
WE'RE ALMOST THERE...
HANG IN THERE, KYLE!

GIRON RAGYUR!!
ZASHOOOM

AGASU ABORUDO !!
GYAAAAA

GRR...
WHAT?! YOU BLOCKED IT?!
YOU LOUSY... I'VE HAD ENOUGH OF PLAYING AROUND...
HOW COULD YOU THWART SOMEONE LIKE ME...
SSSS

DO YOU KNOW WHAT I'M GOING TO DO TO YOU?!!
RRRRK

RGH! ZATCH!!
YEAH!
FWIP
HUH?

POOM

THAT'S RIGHT.
SHF...
WE'RE GOING TO DO THIS TOGE-THER.

YOU'RE GOING TO PROTECT ZATCH, RIGHT?
LET'S TRY *THAT* SPELL. NO MERE DEFENSIVE SPELL WILL BLOCK HIS NEXT ONE.

YOU CAN STAND ON YOUR OWN TWO FEET NOW.
YOU WERE ABLE TO STAND UP AND FACE THAT SCARY MAMODO...
ZAWOOOO

NOW YOU'LL BE OKAY WITHOUT ME.
YOU CAN STAND UP TO ANYBODY.

MII...
MII...
...

DIOGA RAGYUR!!
THANK YOU...
REIN.

YOU'RE WEL-COME, KYLE.
IT'S BEEN FUN.

GARBADOS ABORODIO !!

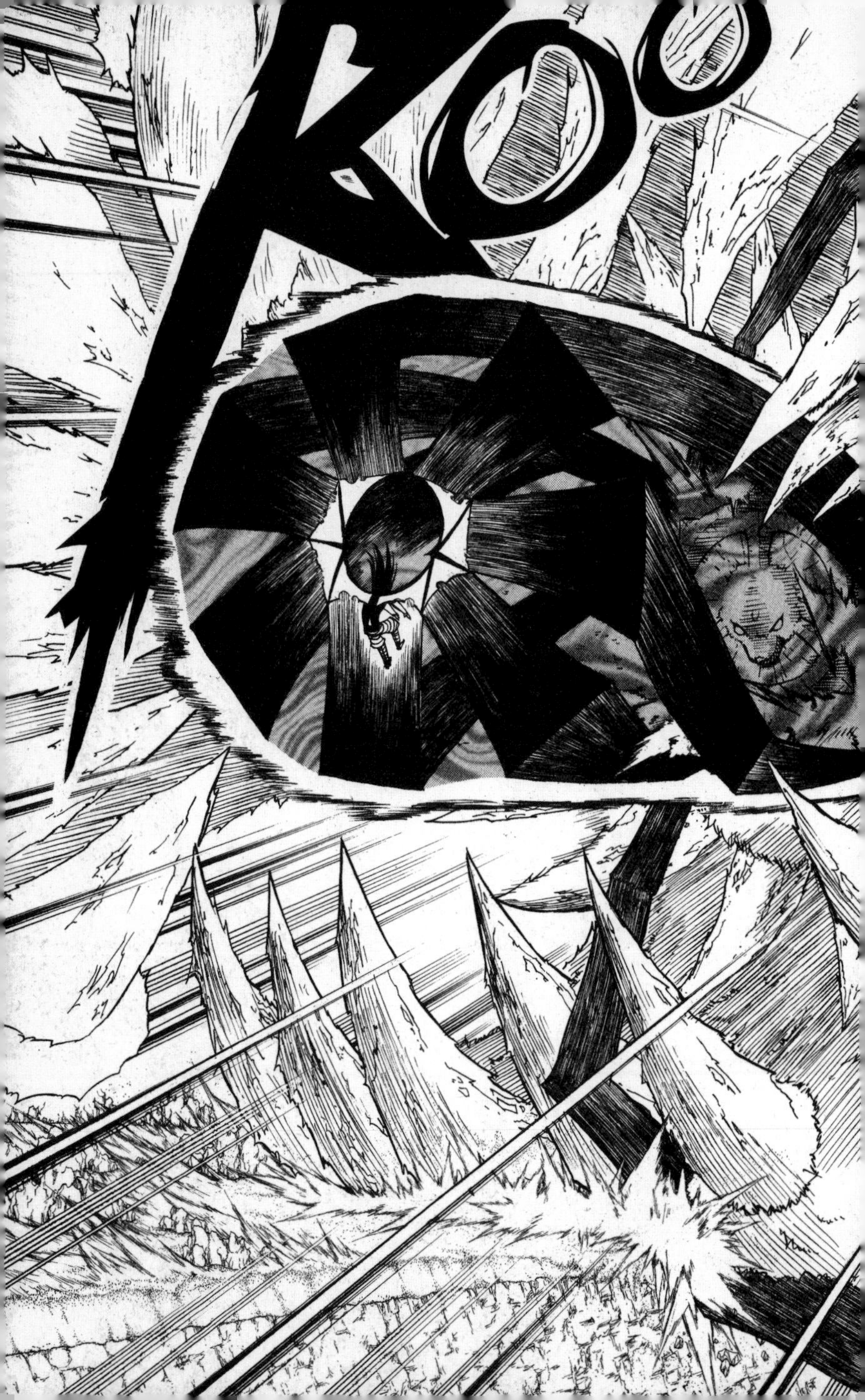
KOO

CURSES!
VSH
CHIIIAAA!!
NGH... NNNH...
SUCH POWER...
G G G G G G

GWAAAAAAAAAAHHHHHHH!
ZGAAAAAAA

HWOOOOOOOOOOO

PHEW

FLOP

AIEEEE!!
COME ON, FASTER! LET'S GET OUT OF HERE!!
SPLASH-SPLASH

W-WOW...
THEY BEAT THEM...
FSSH

!!

NO...
NOT YET...?

GHH...
KA KLUNK
IF ONLY I HAD THAT POWER...

UN-BELIEVABLE! CHIITA SHIELDED HERSELF UNDER RODEAUX, AND DUG A HOLE UNDER-GROUND!
LOOK OUT, ZATCH!
BAMM

DON'T WORRY ...
HE CAN'T FIGHT ANYMORE. THEY CAN BARELY WALK OUT OF HERE.

ANYWAY, THANK YOU, ZATCH...

KYLE CAN STAND ON HIS OWN NOW.

I HAVE...
...NO REGRETS ANYMORE.
TO BE CONTINUED!!

*BUFFALOMAN IS A CHARACTER FROM YUDETAMAGO'S MANGA *ULTIMATE MUSCLE*.

SO, EVERY-BODY...
HOW DO YOU DRAW MANGA WITHOUT MAKING A HOLE ON YOUR SLEEVE?
LIFT UP YOUR ARM AS YOU DRAW...?
OH YEAH, WE CAN USE "THOSE THINGS."
"THOSE THINGS"?
YOU KNOW... BUFFALO-MAN'S ARM THINGIES.

OH, THOSE!!
YES, THE THINGS THAT BUFFALOMAN WEARS ON HIS ARMS...
These
...NOT TO MENTION SCHOOLTEACHERS, CLERKS, AND SO ON.
These

ALL RIGHT, LET'S GO BUY SOME!
SO, GUYS, WHERE CAN I GET THOSE?

DO YOU KNOW, MR. OKUBO?
EH?
WHY DON'T YOU ASK BUFFALO-MAN TO SELL YOU HIS?
HOW ABOUT YOU, MR. KURO-DA?
I HAVE A WONDERFUL SISTER AND A DOG!
Ha ha ha! what do you think of that?

*AKIBA=AKIHABARA, TOKYO'S FAMOUS ELECTRONICS DISTRICT

ZATCH AND SKY
by Makoto Raiku

DOOOM

BOOOM

SUNBEAM GOT US THESE CRAB AND HAWK MASKS FROM HOKKAIDO...
WHAT SHOULD WE DO WITH THEM?

KEEE KEEE KEEE!
BAT
BAT
CHIKA CHIKA CHIKA!

MAKOTO RAIKU

Happy New Year! This is my fifth year writing *Zatch Bell!* and it's all thanks to you readers. I'll work harder than ever, so please stick around.

ZATCH BELL!
Vol. 19

STORY AND ART BY
MAKOTO RAIKU

Translation/David Ury
Touch-up Art & Lettering/Annaliese Christman
Design/Courtney Utt
Special Thanks/Kit Fox, Izumi Hirayama, Jessica Villat,
Miki Macaluso, Mitsuko Kitajima, and Akane Matsuo
Editor/Jason Thompson

Editor in Chief, Books/Alvin Lu
Editor in Chief, Magazines/Marc Weidenbaum
VP of Publishing Licensing/Rika Inouye
VP of Sales/Gonzalo Ferreyra
Sr. VP of Marketing/Liza Coppola
Publisher/Hyoe Narita

Printed in the U.S.A.

Published by VIZ Media, LLC
P.O. Box 77010
San Francisco, CA 94107

10 9 8 7 6 5 4 3 2 1
First printing, June 2008

www.viz.com
store.viz.com